END

Ryan has a unique and compelling story to tell, and his life has been an adventurous journey! I first got to know Ryan when we wrote "Speak Life" together. Now I know him as a friend and an artist. I am truly impacted by who he is as a person and thankful we now walk together through this world. Ryan cares deeply about the things that matter, and he lives them out with passion. I am truly blessed to call him friend.

—**TobyMac**, award-winning artist and producer

Ryan's story is captivating and unique—nothing short of miraculous! I loved reading about his journey and seeing the Lord's hand on his life. This is a beautifully compelling story, and I'm excited to see what the future holds for him.

—**Bart Millard**, lead singer for Mercy Me

Ryan is deeply committed to the honesty of the journey. I am honored to be a witness to his courage and determination and his wholehearted pursuit of authentic truth-telling and creative craft.

—**Paul Young**, bestselling author of *The Shack*

Ryan is quite possibly one of the best storytellers I've ever had the good pleasure to work with. From the moment I met him and we talked for nearly three hours on the couch of my office, he mesmerized me with the tale of his journey. I know we listened to music at some point in that meeting, but it was *this* story you're about to read that I remember most in that first meeting. Ryan is an amazing musician, songwriter, and performer, but I think God gave him that Mark Twain quality of telling a tale that seems so familiar yet so fantastical that you're not sure if fact is fiction or fiction is fact, but you know that you just can't put the book down.

—**Joey Elwood**, president and cofounder of Gotee Records

Our family and Ryan's go back many years. His mother and I became best friends, so our families ended up spending a lot of time together. His musical abilities did not start coming out until he left for college, so who could have known that he would end up where he is? Only God! We are proud of him and his success. He will always remain one of our kids.

—**Sandy DeJong**, owner of Langell Valley Dairy

Ryan Stevenson literally saved my life with his abilities as a paramedic, his value for the sanctity of life itself, and most importantly…prayer. Within these pages lie not only stories about Ryan's journey but also messages of hope, persistence, and love that will become a part of your soul. I have a special place in my heart for Ryan, and I believe that once you get to know him through his story, you'll make a place for him in yours as well.

—**Lara Eusterman**, lightning strike survivor

EYE OF THE STORM

RYAN STEVENSON

HARVEST HOUSE PUBLISHERS
EUGENE, OREGON

Cover design by Faceout Studio

Interior design by KUHN Design Group

Eye of the Storm

Published by Harvest House Publishers
Eugene, Oregon 97408
www.harvesthousepublishers.com

ISBN 978-0-7369-7977-1 (pbk.)
ISBN 978-0-7369-7978-8 (eBook)

Library of Congress Cataloging-in-Publication Data is on file at the Library of Congress, Washington, DC.

Printed in the United States of America

20 21 22 23 24 25 26 27 28 / VP-SK / 10 9 8 7 6 5 4 3 2 1

CONTENTS

FOREWORD

It is my pleasure to introduce you to Ryan Stevenson, though for many of you he really needs no introduction. You'll likely remember precisely where you were when you first heard his stomp-and-clap anthem, "Eye of the Storm." I was speaking at an event in Klamath Falls, Oregon, when I heard a local choir sing the song, and it sent a few shivers down my spine.

Many of you also know Ryan as a songwriter who has produced a litany of Billboard hit singles and the Grammy-nominated song "Speak Life," which he co-wrote. Of course, you likely have seen him perform in a stadium with the Christian pop king, TobyMac, who has anointed him as his heir apparent. Frankly, if you listen to the radio as you drive, you seemingly can't go fifteen minutes without hearing one of his songs.

Accolades apply.

Though Ryan may be known for the *breadth* of his reach, it is the *depth* of his reach that I find most staggering. I never told Ryan about this (well, until now!), but I recently spoke in Eugene, Oregon, and afterward a sweet little country girl came forward to be baptized. When the pastor asked her why, she said that she sometimes just sits in her room crying because she loves God so much…and that one particular song always brings these tears to her eyes: "The Gospel" by Ryan Stevenson.

In fact, her eyes filled with tears just *thinking* about what the song does to her.

Ryan isn't all treble and no bass. He doesn't just skim. He takes you deep. He doesn't just fill arenas. He changes lives. And his uncanny prowess for touching people's hearts comes from the fact that his own has been broken. He has journeyed into the eye of the storm and lived to tell the tale.

Now that Ryan and I have both written books, it strikes me how parallel our journeys have been. Over the last year we've been on TV and radio together and have shared the stage in front of thousands of people. But when I first met him, I was just a rube from southern Oregon battling suicidal depression, and he was doing shows for 30 kids in the middle of nowhere, trying to keep his head above water.

Ryan was a starving artist who couldn't catch a break. Most people in his sneakers would have given up. But he is made of different stuff. He is from the tiny burg of Bonanza, Oregon, which tells you most of what you need to know. His hard-nosed, stoic, heroic, tempered-steel personality was forged in his seminal years as a paramedic. His regular mode of transportation then was not a tour bus, but an ambulance. He experienced blood, sweat, and tears literally every day. Having survived these experiences, he was prepared for anything that the music business might throw at him.

Most singer-songwriters, though, would have packed up their skinny jeans and gotten a job at Verizon. But though Ryan had bags—well, more like suitcases—under his eyes, he kept on carrying his own when there seemed little hope. He converted situations that were painful into pain fuel, and he kept traveling with his guitar in hand to one little Podunk town after the other.

He kept playing his music, even when it felt like a Herculean task. And now he is beloved for his soulful melodies and happy-clappy vibes.

Ryan is childlike in the very best definition of that word. And it takes a strong person to go through the things he has gone through and not lose the joy in living. He is living proof that the fire doesn't burn you, it forges you. God, the consuming fire, is not about burning you, but about burning away everything that isn't you! Now Ryan is busy carrying buckets of water for those who feel like they are being consumed by the flames of their lives.

Ryan doesn't so much say, "Hear my words," as, "Touch my wounds."

You'll find his story one you can't easily put down. He shows in these pages that his gift with words extends beyond songwriting. In them you'll discover what he has found to be true: The storm cannot take you where the eye of God cannot see you.

—***Ben Courson***
October 11, 2019

I don't disassociate from that history; I am an expression of it... [God] doesn't deny our brokenness...or deny our participation in darkness. He takes all of that, and by redeeming it, weaves it into the sound that we now become, and so that it is present with us in the moment... [Our past is] too precious to lock it into a memory.

WILLIAM PAUL YOUNG[1]

PREFACE

Over the years, when people have heard my story they've often told me, "You need to write a book." Honestly, I never gave that much thought. Writing a book seemed like an Everest I had very little interest in climbing. It seemed a little scary and would require me to be a lot more vulnerable than I thought I wanted to be.

Sometimes, though, it is good to do something scary, so I've done it. As I wrote these pages, I remembered what a pastor friend once told me: "Always err on the side of vulnerability, because vulnerability creates more trust, not less." With that in mind, I have written the tale of my own life, with all its unexpected twists and turns. And the hero of the story isn't me, but the One who is the author of all our stories.

Many times it has been difficult to recognize the Lord's hand in the middle of my unfolding circumstances. Many times it felt like the storm was too strong and beyond my strength to get through. Many times it was the transitional moments, when the storm rose around me, that I discovered the greatest temptation for disobedience and fear. And many times I have just had to hold on for dear life. But I always discovered that, in the midst of the storm, God was holding on to me.

Whenever I tried to hold on to what I thought was most important, I only found deeper realms of confusion. It was in letting go that I was finally able to see the purpose of the winds that roared around me, which were only there to carry me up into a higher realm and a different perspective. From there I could more clearly see the purposes God had in store for me.

One of my favorite pastors, Damon Thompson, said, "The greatest tool of evangelism is not just the gospel message contained within the Scriptures, but it's the gospel message connected to your story." In other words, our testimony is a way of setting ourselves and others free.

So here you have my imperfect attempt to do just that. To tell my story with as much honesty and vulnerability as I can. From it I hope you'll take away this one great truth, the truth that has changed my life and given me the strength to face every difficult thing that has come my way (including writing this book!): In the middle of all your struggles, failures, and heartaches, God will never leave you to face the pain alone. You can never be separated from His love.

That's the story that sets us all free.

In my case, it goes something like this...

PROLOGUE

IN THE BELLY OF THE BLUE AND WHITE

There have been moments in my life when I've felt like I was right in the middle of a storm: times when uncertainty, chaos, and confusion raged around me, and it was hard to see beyond the threatening black clouds of fear.

There have been other times in my life when the storm I faced was quite literal. One of these moments set events in motion that would change the course of my life.

Several years ago I was working as a paramedic in Boise, Idaho, and it was a typical October day. The sky was blue, and the sunshine was abundant. The temperature was moderately warm, which was the norm for that time of year. Despite the beautiful weather, I couldn't shake the thought that something felt unsettled in the atmosphere.

It was three o'clock. I had just finished up a run to the hospital to deliver a patient with my paramedic partner, Randall. We'd signaled ourselves as "out of service" so that the dispatch team wouldn't assign us to take another call while we were completing the last one. Now we thoroughly cleaned out the back of our ambulance, as I liked to keep the vehicle spick and span. We'd already been working for eight hours and had responded to several emergency situations that day, but since we worked on a rotating shift of 24 hours, we still had another 16 to go. We were scheduled to work through the night and not get off until the next morning.

At that point we decided we needed a quick break, so we went to grab a cup of coffee from the gas station across the street from the emergency room. Perhaps it reveals something you should know about me that I would just as soon have a cup of coffee from a gas station, with some hazelnut creamer added, rather than some fancy concoction made by a high-class barista. I was raised with simple tastes, and I still hold on to them.

Sipping my coffee, I thought about where I was at this point in my life. At 28 years old, I had been a paramedic for nearly six years and felt like I was pretty good at my job. I had already experienced countless bizarre and heart-wrenching situations during the innumerable calls I had answered as a medic. And I had learned to deal with the stress and surprises that come with the territory. I thought I had reached an emotional state where nothing could possibly faze me. To survive, I needed to be able to shake off the disturbing moments. I couldn't dwell on the horrifying scenes I stumbled upon or I'd risk my own mental health.

By this time, frankly, I thought I had seen it all. But I couldn't have guessed what I was about to encounter that very day.

Realizing we needed to refuel the ambulance, Randall and I headed for the fueling station with our hot coffee in hand. Since refueling sometimes took a few minutes, we put the ambulance out of service again while we filled the tank with diesel. We both commented on the strange feeling in the atmosphere but knew that the weather at this time of year could often be unpredictable. Once the tank was full, we headed back toward our station on the west side of Boise.

Randall was driving, and I was in the passenger seat, which meant that I was responsible for taking the next call. It was also my job to operate our MDT (mobile data terminal), which we could use to map the location of where we needed to go. We were shooting the breeze and finishing up the last of our coffee when the weather took a strange and unexpected turn. Suddenly, the sky went black and dark storm clouds rolled in. Out of nowhere a thunder and lightning storm kicked up, and a torrential rain began to pound down on the ambulance. Randall had to slow down to a crawl because he couldn't see very well out the windshield.

The storm was disconcerting. I'd grown up in the Pacific Northwest, so I was accustomed to rain—but this was different. It was fierce and furious and threatening. Then, almost as quickly as it came, it passed over us. The black clouds lifted, and the sun popped its face back out, almost as if it were saying with a smirk, "Okay, I'm back."

The steam started rising off the blacktop as the warmth of the sun evaporated the fresh coating of fallen rain. And then our radio made its four distinctive beeping sounds, and the dispatcher announced a lightning strike on Hidden Springs Road, near the dump. We were much nearer than the unit she was dispatching to the scene, and Randall and I realized we had failed to put our vehicle "back in service" after we had stopped for fuel. So I got on the radio and responded, letting them know that we'd handle this one. Randall hit the lights and siren, and away we flew, white and blue—past the fairgrounds, over the river, and up into the foothills.

I couldn't believe we were responding to a lightning strike. That was a new one. Dispatch returned on the radio once again to give a full update. "Medic Fifty-Six, lightning strike, 39-year-old female, code blue." I began visualizing the scene in my head, mentally preparing how I would handle this call, as I would be the paramedic in charge.

As we were driving, I turned to Randall. "So, have you ever seen a lightning strike before?"

Randall, being the calm and composed veteran he always was, casually scrolled through his mental Rolodex and responded, "Nope, but I've seen someone die after being electrocuted. It was a guy who lifted an aluminum water pipe up into some power lines that he didn't see above him."

I didn't want to dwell on that visual image.

Nothing I had experienced in my six years as a paramedic prepared me for what I was about to see.

As we wound our way up Hidden Springs Road, we could see the chaotic scene up ahead. There was a fire truck with red lights revolving, the sheriff's vehicle, and an SUV, as well as a few other cars belonging to those who had stopped out of curiosity or to try to lend a hand. They were all gathered around the victim, who was lying about 50 feet off the side of the road.

We climbed out of our unit and made our way over to the scene. There was an older woman standing nearby, her eyes filled with terror and confusion, tears streaming down her face. An Ada County sheriff's deputy was standing beside the SUV, trying to comfort two small boys who appeared stunned and shaken. Everybody looked wet, and I remembered the freak downpour that had occurred just a few minutes earlier.

The victim, a 39-year-old woman, was stretched out on her back on a grassy slope of the Boise foothills. She was drenched with rain, and all the color had left her body. She wasn't moving. By the appearance of her skin and the overpowering stench of burnt hair, I quickly surmised that she had been flash-burned by the electrical storm.

It didn't take but a minute to come to grips with the fact that this lady wasn't going to make it. I ached for the boys who had to be her two young sons. They sat in the car only a few feet away and couldn't avoid observing this graphic scene. I wanted to protect them from seeing their mama lying dead in such a horrific state, so we moved her from the grass and placed her in the back of the ambulance so we could transport her to the hospital, and, for all the good I thought it would do, at least administer CPR en route.

I took a seat on the chair in the back of the ambulance, near the woman's head. She had no heartbeat and could not breathe on her own. I figured she had been lifeless for about ten minutes. The smell of burnt flesh and fresh blood rose from her body and permeated the back of the ambulance. The situation seemed so hopeless. I took a deep breath and prayed for guidance, asking the Lord to keep me calm and strengthen me to help this woman to the best of my ability. But I really didn't think there was anything I could do. It was just too late.

Our ambulance sped along the winding roads, and everything around me swayed back and forth haphazardly. I had a hard time keeping my balance in the chair. With every jerk, turn, and acceleration the IV lines hanging from the hooks and railing above me swung, sometimes hitting me in the face. I was surrounded by a chaotic mess of bandages, IV catheters, oxygen tubing, airway tools, an EKG cardiac monitor, and a bag-valve mask—everything needed for an emergency situation. But at the moment it seemed that this was *beyond* an emergency.

I tried to mentally rehearse all the lifesaving protocols I knew. I was absolutely stressed and trying to figure out what to do next, but I felt a strange sense of calm and knew that God was there with us in the back of that ambulance.

Present in the eye of the storm.

Just 20 minutes prior it had been another routine day at work, but now here I was in the back of the ambulance with this young woman whose life was slipping away. I didn't know how I could help her. At this point, I didn't really think she could be saved.

As I slid a breathing tube into her lungs and inserted needles into her arms, I realized that the people in all the cars we were passing had no idea of the drama unfolding inside this EMT unit as a woman was at the very precipice of death. They never could have imagined it.

Nor could I have imagined that this encounter with the victim of a lightning strike would eventually change the course of my life.

CHAPTER 1

SUPER BOWL BABY

It was a snowy morning on January 21, 1979—Super Bowl Sunday. My mom snapped awake when her water broke. I was just about ready to enter this world. She shook my dad awake and frantically shouted for him to take her to the hospital. He loaded her into their old, beat-up pickup and navigated the 20-mile distance as fast as he could along slick, icy roads to get her to Merle West Medical Center in Klamath Falls, Oregon. I was born an hour later.

One afternoon, while taking a leisurely drive in the country outside of Klamath Falls, Mom and Dad had discovered Bonanza, Oregon—an unassuming little town with a population of 250. They immediately took to the vibe of the community and both felt drawn to the area. So they bought a plot of land there with money from Dad's GI loan and had enough left over to purchase a little 940-square-foot single-wide trailer. They dug a well, set up their mobile home on cinder blocks, and began a new life in Bonanza. This would be the place where I would live out my formative years.

Dad came from a long line of hillbillies from Tennessee and Arkansas who had originally migrated from Ireland. My dad was born in the humid summer of July 1947 in Atkins, Arkansas, the fourth of six children. He was literally "born in a barn." I know because I saw the very horse stall where this momentous event occurred when we visited there years later during my junior year of high school.

Their home was totally off the beaten track, tucked away in a grassy, wooded field miles away from civilization of any sort. Dad still tells stories about his dad riding a horse to work, his mom shooting squirrels for their meals, and him never having shoes for his feet. You could say they were poor, but they were happy. When times got hard, his parents moved out to the Oregon coast in search of work, and Grandpa got a job at a lumber mill in Garibaldi, Oregon.

My mom had a rather different introduction to the world. She was essentially the product of a statutory rape and had been put up for adoption by her mother, who had given birth at age 17. In those days unwed pregnant girls were typically sent away in order to give birth in secret at the home of a relative to avoid any disgrace to their families. Mom's birth mother, Charlene, was sent to the home of an aunt and uncle in Vancouver, Washington.

When the time for Mom's arrival came, Charlene was busy pushing her daughter into the world while just down the hall a young couple was experiencing their third stillbirth. The doctor entered the room of this couple and told them that a young lady down the hall had just given birth to a baby girl and was planning to give her up. Did they want her?

There was no hesitation. They took home my mom, and that wonderful couple became my grandparents. They moved to the Oregon coast when Mom was still small. In fact, my parents met as children in Rockaway Beach, Oregon, and stayed in touch here and there during their childhood. When it came time for them to graduate high school, my dad suddenly started to look at my mom in a new way.

Dad joined the navy after graduation and did his basic training in San Diego. He was then stationed in Key West, Florida, followed by Sasebo, Japan, before being deployed to Cam Ranh Bay in Vietnam. He served two years in the Vietnam War, which left him with a lot of interesting stories, but also with a residual impact from what he saw during his time there. He never fully recovered from what he had witnessed in the jungles of Vietnam.

Returning from the war, Dad found that my mom had grown into a beautiful young woman, and he soon fell deeply in love. To impress her he bought a metallic cherry-red 1967 Chevelle Super Sport and began pursuing her in earnest. Soon, they were engaged.

My parents were married on September 15, 1973, in Rockaway Community Church, where they were active members. It was the same small church in which they had grown up together. My older sister, Janay, was born two years later, and they soon decided it was time for a change of scenery. They packed up their belongings and put them in the back of their 1978 Ford pickup, which had replaced the sporty red car. They filled it up to the top of the wooden side rails, secured the items with a green tarp, and made the drive to Klamath Falls. My dad had been offered a job falling timber there. So with an open road, very little money, and an uncertain future, they left the coast and headed for south-central Oregon in search of a fresh start.

Though they didn't know it at the time, I was an unexpected fellow traveler—a bun in the oven.

CHAPTER 2

SINGLE-WIDE DREAMIN'

You never really understand how small your house is when you're young. Even though we lived in a trailer that was less than 1,000 square feet, it seemed huge to me when I was a kid. My sister and I each had our own rooms, so I never realized how cramped for space we were until I got older. My mother's tendency to collect things didn't help. She was a bit of an obsessive when it came to cleanliness and extremely organized...but she was also, for all practical purposes, a class-two hoarder. Though our house was always spotless, there was some form of budget decor in nearly every nook and cranny. She vacuumed the floor every day, keeping it so clean you could eat a meal off it. Then she would gracefully move through the house, humming hymns as she dusted, moved furniture, adjusted the angles of the pictures on the walls, and precisely repositioned her countless little knickknacks.

My family had settled in Bonanza, which is nestled in the foothills of the Cascade Range in south-central Oregon. It's only about 15 miles north of the California border, and as far as you drive in every direction, you'll discover gorgeous landscapes of green alfalfa fields, blue lakes, rivers, rolling hills, and towering mountains. It's like stepping into a Van Gogh painting. During the summer evenings, we'd sit on the back porch, drinking sun tea and chatting well into the night with our neighbors. Before the sun disappeared behind the hills we could hear the soothing rumble of farm equipment in the fields, stuttering wheel lines watering the crops, and cows begging for their evening feeding.

In this small farming community, there was only one school, which serviced all the grades from kindergarten through twelfth. We also had a post office, two gas stations, a general store, and a seedy little saloon called The Longhorn. There was only one doctor and one dentist for the town. They shared a workspace in a single-wide trailer behind the post office. Each had an "office" at one end of the trailer. Sometimes, while getting my physical exam for sports, I could hear the drilling of a cavity being filled.

Big Springs Park is at the edge of town. This was the place where my friends and I would spend countless hours traipsing along the muddy riverbanks, catching frogs, and fishing. Natural spring water is abundant in the park, and we could literally drink right out of the ground as the water bubbled up. I remember how cold and refreshing it was on hot days. It's the abundance of water in the area that makes the surrounding land in the valley extremely fertile—perfect for farming.

A rural farming community like this is a mecca for exploration, and as a young boy, I became well acquainted with everything in the outdoors. Hunting, fishing, hiking, and camping were my top priorities, though I couldn't legally hunt until I was 12. Still, my dad would sometimes take me out to the fields, where we would shoot squirrels and rodents. He taught me to drive on one of these outings, turning me loose in his brown 1969 GMC pickup while we were trapping gophers in the fields.

By the age of 11, I was competent with a stick shift, though I had to put pillows under my bottom in order to see over the steering wheel. When I turned 12, I took a hunter safety course and got my license to hunt for big game. This was a big deal since hunting was my family's annual ritual, and hunting season was the most anticipated time of year for us.

In a small community like Bonanza there are essentially two classes of people: the wealthy land owners, who are ranchers and farmers, and the people who work for them. It didn't take me long to figure out where I stood on the social ladder. My parents could never afford the popular name-brand clothes for my sister and me. Since my self-image was tied up in my appearance, having to wear the generic brands of clothing and shoes cemented my identity as a social outcast.

I only felt like I fit in around my family and closest friends. But these relationships weren't always smooth. I could sense the ever-present stress, which was rooted in the facts that we never had enough money to make ends meet and Mom's health was never good. The arguments between my parents usually centered around these two issues. They were either arguing about money or arguing about why Mom wasn't sticking to her diet.

My dad didn't earn a lot of money as a farmhand, and my mom had a dangerous "feast or famine" spending mentality. If any extra money was available, she would race off to town and spend it, stocking up on supplies we didn't really need. Upon her return from town, like clockwork, she and my dad would begin their routine arguments about money. All this only confirmed the truth of what I most dreaded—that I was "poor white trash."

I hated the time when Christmas would roll around every year. It unfailingly reminded me of just how low on the totem pole I was in relation to my peers, so I loathed it unlike anything else. Because of my family's deep roots in our faith and church, I understood the true meaning of Christmas, but that didn't keep me from being worried about going back to school after the Christmas break, which was when everyone else would proudly display all the stuff they had received.

I always found myself timidly shuffling down the "catwalk," on display for all to see, with nothing special to model. All the other kids had received the kind of clothes that I had wished for but knew I was never going to have. And I felt guilty that even the modest gifts I'd received had clearly been a weight upon the family finances. In the run-up to Christmas I would usually overhear my parents talking about the need to borrow money to buy presents. Somehow, Christmas morning always seemed to happen, and Mom and Dad always seemed to come through with the best gifts they could scrape together. But the gifts weren't usually the kind that invested me with the social status I longed for.

The way each of my parents handled the stress of our financial hardships couldn't have been more different. My dad was always humble and unassuming, refusing to give off the slightest impression that he was stressed. He was a hard worker who would not refuse any work offered him, and he never wanted a handout. He held his cards tight to his chest and rarely showed much emotion around me.

My mom, on the other hand, was an open book. She wore her emotions on the surface and didn't hesitate to tell me that she didn't know what they were going to do about their finances. The phone rang off the hook with calls from collection agencies, and our mail always seemed to be full of bills—most of them of the "past due" and "final notice" variety. I remember my mother telling me at one point that she thought we might lose the house because of their inability to make a $300 house payment. Hearing this news from my mom shattered nearly every ounce of security I had.

We didn't have a lot, but one thing I was sure of was that we had each other. That may sound like some sort of cliché, but it wasn't. What we didn't have monetarily we had emotionally and spiritually. My mom might not have been good with money, but she was very spiritually sensitive and had a remarkable gift for caring and nurturing. She solidified in me the belief that the desires of my heart were there for a special reason. She encouraged me to follow wherever the Lord was leading me, to always listen to the nudges from that still, small voice inside. This was a lesson that shaped my life, and I still carry it with me. No matter how bad things might be at times, I always know that I have a connection with a God who wants to walk with me through every circumstance.

Whenever life became overwhelming, and every time I was reminded that I didn't fit in, I had a place where I could go and escape from the pain and embarrassment of feeling like an outcast: my little room in that single-wide trailer. I could retreat to my bedroom and dream about my future. I'd envision myself someday becoming a famous athlete or—even more exciting to imagine—a popular musician.

Sometimes I would grab a few pots and pans from the kitchen, along with a couple mismatched wooden spoons, and climb up to my top bunk, where I'd set up a makeshift drum set, playing along to a cassette tape from Wham. With George Michael in my ear as I banged on those pots and pans, I discovered a love and passion for music. This, I thought, was more than a hobby—it was something to which I wanted to devote my life.

There at the end of the block, where the pavement stopped, was a young man coming of age in a little tan single-wide. My low-income circumstances may not have cultivated confidence, but they did cultivate a dreamer.

CHAPTER 3

HOLSTEIN HEAVEN

When I think about the things that have shaped me into the person I am today, one of the most important was the time I spent working on a dairy farm, my very own Holstein heaven.

My mom attended a Bible study with a fiery, larger-than-life Dutch lady named Sandy DeJong, who became her best friend. Sandy and her family would become very important in my own life as well. Sandy and her husband, Bill, owned a small dairy farm six miles outside of Bonanza. My first real job was working with them.

Sandy was one of the most amazing people I've ever known—a big, bursting personality, full of kindness and compassion toward everyone she met. She was ready to take in every stray that crossed her path, whether it be a dog, a cat, or a needy human being like me. She was the very personification of no-nonsense kindness. She wasn't really that concerned about things like cussing or engaging in a bit of boyish mischief, though if you ticked her off she wasn't afraid to let you know. Her pet peeve was when the boys would make a mess and not clean it up. But no matter what stupid thing we might have done, she would always be there for us.

Her husband was a serious man, as stern as Sandy was tolerant. But he was always fair, and he was an incredible judge of character. He was born in Holland and had come to the United States with his family at age four. He retained a lot of his Dutch heritage. If you were out of line, he'd let you know without a moment's hesitation. Just a glance at him—the way he stood, the way he walked, the massive calluses on his hands, and that subtle scowl of concentration that rose on his face whenever he spoke—these let you know it wasn't a good idea to push his buttons. The thing that rankled him most was any sign of laziness and dishonesty, and even the slightest whiff of deceit would rile him up.

Bill took his work as seriously as he took everything else. Just one hour working alongside him would purge the sloth right out of you. He didn't coddle you either. He was perfectly happy to let you learn a hard lesson from experience, especially if he thought it would rid you of a sense of entitlement. For me, the bottom line was that he was a truly good man. He inspired both fear if I goofed off and a sense of settled peace if I was responsible.

I thought at the time that their oldest daughter, Susie, was the most beautiful girl I had ever seen—a lovely Dutch girl with a fierce, bold, and passionate disposition. It took no time at all for me to develop a huge crush on her, and I hoped that someday she'd realize I was her soul mate and fall in love with me in return. That, of course, never happened.

Her younger brother, Richard, became my best friend. The middle brother, Willem, was the smart one, with a quick wit and an answer for every question, but also a touch of that middle-child insecurity. He always seemed to teeter between taking sides with either Richard or Susie, depending on whom he wasn't getting along with that day.

When I first met Richard, I knew he would be my best friend for life. He was a muscular guy with a perfectly chiseled physique, like some sort of miniature Greek god. He was so deeply tanned from working out in the sun that when I was introduced to him, I thought maybe he was a black kid whom the family had adopted. He was strong and honest. He considered loyalty to be just about the most important quality a person could have, and injustice in any form drove him crazy. He wasn't afraid of hard work, and his passion was the dairy farm. His maturity was well beyond what was typical for his age, and he had an unfailing willingness to shoulder tremendous responsibility. Truly, he was a good guy to have in my life. Once we met, we quickly became inseparable.

My parents had no problem letting me spend as much time at the dairy as I wanted because they believed it was good for me. I think it was mostly because they knew I'd be outside, working hard, staying busy, and keeping out of trouble. Plus, they were convinced that Richard and his family would be a good influence on me. And they were.

I loved the dairy. I remember when I saw it for the first time. The green pastures stretched out as far as I could see, filled with black-and-white Holstein cows peacefully grazing. I loved it all: the barns and farm equipment, the corrals and ponds, and even the various pungent smells, like manure and cattle feed. It was total and delightful stimulation overload.

I soon found myself assimilating to the traditions of the DeJongs and the other Dutch families who had settled in the Bonanza area. They all seemed to be related somehow. Many of the adults had been children in Europe and had lived through the Nazi invasion during World War II. Their families had fled to America and eventually settled in rural Oregon. The Dutch were good people—passionate about the priorities of family and work, but also able to throw a great party. Their zeal for life was contagious. I was regularly exposed to traditional Dutch icons such as windmills, tulips, and their fashionable wooden shoes. I also learned a handful of Dutch words and phrases, though many of them were crass and inappropriate. (A young boy learning a new language usually picks up the swear words native speakers use. I would never dare speak their equivalent in English at home!) Most of all, I loved their food. Dutch pastries and desserts were unlike anything I'd ever tasted.

I was the poor kid who was usually self-conscious about the social status of my family. The DeJongs were wealthy by comparison, but they never made me feel like I was different or less than they were. They absorbed me just as I was, treating me like one of their own. I felt a deep sense of belonging when I was around them. They even included me on some of their family trips and outings. Eventually, I was at their home more often than my own, so Sandy provided me with my own little dresser upstairs where I could keep some clothes.

A dairy never sleeps. There is always work to be done. The cows needed to be milked twice each day, 365 days a year. It's a never-ending cycle.

At the DeJongs' dairy, the milkers worked in 12-hour shifts—one beginning at eight o'clock in the morning and ending at eight o'clock at night, and the other beginning at eight at night until eight the next morning. Richard and I did a bunch of the jobs that were necessary to keep that cycle running smoothly. Every morning, we'd wake up to the sound of Bill's booming voice echoing up the stairs: "Boys, wake up! It's six o'clock." We'd reluctantly roll out of bed and put on our work clothes and rubber boots. Depending on the time of year, we'd either head across the street to feed 400 calves or we'd head out to the pastures to move the irrigation pipes.

If we were feeding calves, we'd give them a warm powdered milk mixture loaded with vitamins and minerals, a sort of baby formula for cows. The calves loved it, so they'd go crazy when they'd hear us coming. After we gave milk to each of them, we'd start again at the beginning, this time feeding them a grain mixture. It would take at least an hour to feed them all, and then we'd return to the calf barn, where we'd begin to wash all the bottles and buckets in a large stainless-steel sink filled with hot, soapy water. It may sound like unpleasant work, but honestly, I didn't mind washing bottles and buckets, especially during the winter when the hot water in the sink felt amazing on my nearly frozen hands.

During the summer season we'd move the irrigation pipes. On those mornings we'd pile onto an old orange three-wheeler or an old 110 trail-bike motorcycle and head out to the pasture, where we'd spend the next hour or so moving the ten large sprinkler guns. These large guns watered the grass and kept it nice and green for grazing.

When this morning routine was finished, it was time for breakfast. We'd return from our work to find Sandy in the kitchen, cooking away. She had several traditional Dutch meals in her repertoire, my favorite being Dutch pancakes, called *pannekoek*, which are kind of like crepes, only less fluffy and light. In fact, they were kind of rubbery and stretchy, but you couldn't beat the taste. Especially if you lathered them up with butter and drowned them in Mrs. Butterworth's maple syrup or covered them with Sandy's homemade strawberry freezer jam. Because we were on a dairy, and there were 30,000 gallons of it just a few feet away, we'd wash it all down with fresh, cold milk right out of the tank. The milk was so fresh and raw that if you let it sit for a few minutes, the cream would literally rise to the top. It was kind of like drinking ice cream! Once a week, as a special treat to accompany our breakfast, Sandy would set out a plate of fresh doughnuts that she'd purchased from the local bakery. I can assure you, nothing beat munching on an apple fritter as we headed back out to work.

After breakfast, we always had a specific job to do. Since Richard and I were younger than the other workers, it seemed we always got stuck with the grunt work. Mostly these mundane chores consisted of chopping thistles and picking rocks. It wasn't fun, but sometimes Bill would let us take our .22-caliber rifles along so we could shoot squirrels while we were working. If we weren't allowed to take our guns, we'd sometimes take a break from chopping or picking and gather water in a bucket from the nearby ditch so we could flush squirrels out of their holes. With us around, one way or the other, the squirrels didn't stand a chance.

The job I hated most was painting the fences. On the dairy, there were seemingly endless miles of wooden fence, and it all needed to be repainted every so often. So sometimes we'd find ourselves spending countless hours in the sweltering heat of summer, slinging gallons of dark red paint onto the posts and rails.

One summer, Richard and I spent almost a whole month spraying thistles. Armed with a big tank of herbicide, which was operated by a small five-horsepower, gas-powered pump attached to a 50-foot hose with a spray nozzle, we'd take turns driving while the other manned the sprayer. The truck we used was an old gray Ford pickup. The windows wouldn't roll up or down, and there was an Eagles cassette permanently stuck in the tape deck. Because the volume button was also broken, every time we started the pickup we were serenaded all day long by a continuous loop of "Hotel California."

Around the dinner table in the evening we'd tell our stories about the events of the day, air our complaints, and receive a little spiritual encouragement from Sandy as we feasted on more Dutch food, which she called "prok," a mixture of mashed-up potatoes, beets, and cabbage. I know that doesn't sound very tasty, but after a while I developed an affinity for it, especially when it was loaded up with fresh butter, fine Dutch salt, and sausage. Since we worked with cows, there was always plenty of hamburger and steak to accompany our meals. The family also raised some pigs so there would be fresh bacon, sausage, and pork chops in the freezer.

I experienced a lot of firsts while I worked at the dairy. I learned how to swim in the DeJongs' pool, how to perform backflips on their trampoline, how to milk a cow, how to herd cattle into a corral, how to properly use a shovel to clean up endless amounts of cow manure, and how to pull a calf into the world if the mother cow was having trouble during labor. I tried my first sample of chewing tobacco, which made me lightheaded and caused me to throw up. I also tried my first cigarette with the other boys inside a four-person pup tent in the backyard. I didn't fare much better with that than with the chewing tobacco. Because several of the farmhands were Mexicans, I learned to speak Spanish pretty well. Working alongside them offered a free opportunity to become bilingual.

Perhaps the most memorable of my "first" experiences occurred on the day I broke my arm. That was a day that would go down in infamy around the dairy. Richard, Willem, and I were out in the field moving irrigation pipes when I lost control and crashed the three-wheeler. I was lackadaisically cruising along and not really paying attention when I drove nose first into a large ditch that was concealed by overgrown grass. I distinctly remember the sensation of flying through the air and landing with a heavy thud on the ground, then tumbling along like a rag doll. The airborne three-wheeler went flipping end over end down the row between the irrigation lines, pieces of metal and plastic debris scattering everywhere. For a moment it looked like its own little self-contained tornado.

Somehow, miraculously, the three-wheeler came to rest right-side up with the engine still revving furiously. I picked myself up from the dirt and dusted myself off, then noticed I had a large, funky dip in my forearm. It looked like a bone was about to pop through the surface of my skin. In complete confusion, I got on the three-wheeler, clutching my increasingly painful arm, and rode over to Willem, who was only a few hundred feet away. He was completely unaware of what had just happened, and I was beside myself and crying—not so much because of the pain but because of the dawning fear that Bill was going to murder me when he found out I had destroyed their one and only three-wheeler. I held out my arm so that Willem could see it and told him I was pretty sure it was broken.

Willem gave it a quick glance and, with an annoyed tone, said, "Oh Ryan, your arm isn't broken. Now, get back over there and finish moving pipe." So, we stayed out in the field and finished moving all the irrigation lines. Thirty minutes later we all piled onto the three-wheeler and headed back to the house. The vehicle was now making a nasty metallic sound of grating and grinding, its handlebars were bent and disfigured, and it was pulling hard to the right. We limped it back to the house. Bill just happened to be sitting right there on the back porch, taking off his boots as we pulled up. The three-wheeler still made that strange sound, but even more insistently.

Seeing Bill, I knew I was just about to meet my fate. I walked right up to him, panicked and wailing, and fell into his arms. To my astonishment, he didn't freak out or get mad. Instead, he just hugged me and said matter-of-factly, "Yeah, you probably need to go to the hospital."

Three hours later I was at the hospital having my bones reset and getting a nice little maroon-colored cast.

Richard and his family left a legacy of hard work, integrity, and respect for others that I've carried with me through the rest of my life. Their values and lifestyle rubbed off on me and taught me never to approach life or work with a lazy attitude. I may have felt out of place at school, but I never felt out of place with them. They were a living illustration of what I have learned to be true about God's approach: complete acceptance and unconditional love. This was a lesson I first learned on a dairy farm, which I will always remember as a little slice of heaven—Holstein heaven.

CHAPTER 4

HOOK, LINE, AND SINKER

There is probably nothing more important to most adolescents than "fitting in." It is a major focus when entering junior high, which is, for most people, one of the hardest periods in life.

I was no different. When I was in elementary school I couldn't depend on wearing the latest clothing as my way to get noticed and accepted, so I focused on sports. I became a very accomplished athlete, one of the best in my class. I seemed to be a natural, and I was a top starter on both the soccer and basketball teams. I was a star on my fifth- and sixth-grade soccer teams, and we won first place in the southern Oregon conference both years. When you consider that our team of "country bumpkins" was going up against the big schools, you'll understand why this was such an accomplishment. I was made team captain for the "Klamath All-Stars," leading my team to a bronze medal in the state tournament. One of my coaches told my parents that he believed I had more potential as an athlete than anyone he'd coached in years.

So I immersed myself in sports. I loved to play, but even more I loved the sense of value, accomplishment, and identity it provided. Being an athlete made me feel like I was someone who mattered, someone who could find my purpose through my athletic prowess. But then something went wrong with my physical development.

Between sixth and seventh grade I stopped growing. When I returned to school for seventh grade I noticed that all my friends had grown taller over the summer. Not me. They had started to sprout facial hair. Not me. Their voices had dropped to a lower register. Not me. They all looked like young men, but I was still trapped in the body of a little boy. The girls had begun to blossom, too, as they hit puberty. Everyone looked more mature. Except me. Because I clearly hadn't experienced puberty yet, I stuck out like a sore thumb—or maybe I should say a sore pinkie. Walking through the hallways of school I noticed that just about everyone was taller than me.

Almost overnight the focus of our conversations changed for my friends. The most common topic wasn't sports anymore. Now everyone was more interested in relationships—in chasing and pursuing girls. Sex was a big deal, and promiscuity was worn like a badge of honor. The guys were all busy comparing. Whoever had the most hookups was the envy of us all. I felt totally out of sync with this big change in priorities. After all, I was still a little kid both physically and emotionally. To be honest, the thought of a physical encounter with a girl scared me to death!

Of course, the locker room became the place I dreaded most. It was where I felt puny in a land of developing giants. When everyone hit the showers, the comparisons began as everybody proudly flaunted their developing bodies. For me, it was just a time to be embarrassed. While my body wasn't growing, my sense of shame was. So, I tried to be inconspicuous, getting dressed in private as quickly as I could. I became a master at the art of changing clothes without getting fully naked, and I completely avoided the showers, choosing to wait until I got home to clean up. After gym or basketball practice I'd wrestle my school clothes back onto my pasty, sweaty, sticky frame and ride out the rest of the day stinking of body odor. By the time I got home I felt kind of like an abused dog that had escaped the pound and was looking for a private spot to lie down and lick my wounds.

I became kind of a loner. Many of my best friends found new status in the popular cliques or by hanging around with the older kids. Everyone was in pursuit of being cool, but I knew I couldn't fit in. I was an underdeveloped and emotionally tentative young man stuck in the body of a little kid. Either I was invisible to everyone or I stuck out in embarrassing ways. There seemed to be no middle ground.

But time is no respecter of persons. After a terrifying experience in seventh grade, eighth grade rolled around, and I still hadn't gone through puberty. I still hadn't grown. The chasm of difference between me and others grew even wider. Painfully aware that there was nothing I could do to change my outcast status, I still tried to earn approval by dressing in the latest trends. But given the financial stresses of my family, this was extremely difficult to accomplish. Still, I tried hard to be at the cutting edge of fashion by doing whatever I could to procure the latest brand-name clothes and shoes. It's how I spent most of the money I earned.

Clothes were a key marker for identity at that age. The goal for all of us was to wear the right brands—Nike, Jordan, Polo, Hilfiger, Bugle Boy, and Quicksilver. Wearing these names showed you had style and could afford to shop at the best stores. If you had to wear generic brands or shop at Payless, Kmart, or Goodwill, you just didn't stand a chance of standing out in a good way. Clothes made the man.

Since I was an avid fan of the San Francisco 49ers, my ultimate desire was to have a black and red starter jacket emblazoned with the team logo. I begged and pleaded for one, but I knew they were extremely expensive. I couldn't imagine my parents really being able to afford one. Still, I wanted one so badly I could barely stand it. If I could show my team loyalty through a stylish 49ers jacket, I just knew it would help change my social outlook.

When Christmas rolled around I approached it with the customary sense of dread and anxiety. The holiday arrived like a relative I didn't want to have to deal with and whom I hoped would not overstay their welcome. I resolved to make the best of it. My family followed our usual tradition of attending church on Christmas Eve, and then afterward we went home to watch a movie, share some snacks, and revel in the meaning of the season. I always felt bad for my parents, who I knew were trying to make it a special time. I have to give them credit for that.

On Christmas morning our habit was to get up and enjoy a breakfast made by my dad. He generally wasn't much of a cook, but he could whip up an awesome breakfast of eggs, fried potatoes, and bacon. Mom was always the last one up, as she was a sound sleeper and had trouble waking up and facing the new day. After about three cups of coffee she would finally be awake enough for us to open presents.

I can still remember Mom sitting in her recliner, sipping coffee and tearing off pieces from her breakfast to feed to the miniature schnauzers perched in her lap. Meanwhile, Dad was in the kitchen, snagging a few cookies or a piece of pie to feed his sweet tooth. In his book it never hurt to have dessert after breakfast. He'd pour a glass of cold milk, wrap the dessert in a paper towel, and then consume it with an unbelievable sense of pleasure. When he was finished he would wipe his mouth with the paper towel and crumple it up, often still holding it in his fist while he watched TV. I think he used paper towels so that he wouldn't have to dirty up a plate.

There was a blanket of snow covering the frozen ground that Christmas morning, and our tree was squeezed into one of the few open areas in our living room. Underneath it was a bunch of presents. When it came time to open them I received the usual stuff—things I needed but wasn't really excited about, like socks and underwear. It was, in other words, a normal Christmas for our financially struggling family. When the supply of presents was exhausted, Dad disappeared into the back room and emerged with a box that hadn't been under the tree. It had my name on it. Puzzled, I tore it open.

There, nestled in a bed of tissue, was the present I wanted more than anything else in the world: the black and red 49ers starter jacket. I was ecstatic. I put it on and didn't remove it for the rest of the day. I'll never know how they managed to pull the money together to purchase something so impractical and extravagant, but frankly, I didn't care at the time. Now I owned the kind of jacket that even the coolest kids aspired to have. Even if I still didn't fit in, at least this jacket would provide a sort of buffer between the social distinctions.

Were we poor? Yes, poor enough that buying a stylish team jacket demanded financial sacrifices. But somehow, I often forgot where we stood on the economic ladder. Until reality occasionally reared its head.

I tried incessantly to reason with myself—telling myself that we weren't really that poor. However, I got a grade A dose of reality one day at the grocery store, solidifying everything I was fighting not to believe. I remember going into town with my mom to pick up a few groceries. She loaded our cart with the essentials and a few things we probably didn't need and took it all to the counter, where the clerk scanned it at the register. When the clerk gave her the total balance owed, I saw her reach into her purse and try to inconspicuously pay with something that looked like cash but clearly wasn't. I knew something was up because she normally paid with a check—usually a post-dated one.

I didn't say anything until we got back in the car, but as she started the engine I asked her, "Mom, what was that you used to pay for the groceries?"

She reached down to put the car into gear, then hesitated as a disgraced look came over her face. With a solemn tone, she told me they were food stamps. "They are for people who need a little help with money. It's just to help us until we can get back on our feet."

That statement tore through me like a knife. For the first time I came to fully understand that we were *poor*. It didn't matter that I had a fancy jacket. I was still an undersized kid from a poor family. I became increasingly despondent, and my sense of inadequacy grew. But I didn't want my friends and family to know how I was feeling, so I tried to make the best of things and deflect the pain that rose from the bullying and mockery of other kids at school. The truth felt indistinguishable from the lies that said I was inadequate and unworthy and didn't have a place in the world, and I believed them all—hook, line, and sinker.

CHAPTER 5

JESUS NORTHWEST

I still remember how excited I was when Sandy DeJong, who was not only my second mom but also the leader of our church youth group, announced that we were all going to drive up to Vancouver, Washington, for a big Christian music festival called Jesus Northwest. With as much as I loved music, this sounded like the perfect way to spend a few summer days.

Jesus Northwest was a Christian version of Woodstock. Lots of music, but without the drugs and debauchery. Each year it attracted thousands of people who came from all over the Pacific Northwest. For our group it meant an eight-hour drive in a crusty old Ford Econoline van that could accommodate 15 passengers. We set up our tents among all the thousands of tents, trailers, campers, and motor homes; unrolled our sleeping bags; and prepared for three full days of music and inspiration from some of our favorite artists, bands, and speakers. The lineup included Michael W. Smith, Newsboys, Petra, and a band whose music I didn't know very well with the unlikely name of DC Talk.

I was especially excited about hearing Petra because they had one of the best drummers in Christian music, a guy named Louie Weaver. He had the quintessential long, blond, rocker hairstyle and could chop it up with his drums better than anyone I knew. By this time, I had become a pretty decent drummer myself, thanks to all those hours in my bedroom pounding on my mom's pots and pans. I'd graduated to a real drum set and had become adept at keeping the beat. Petra also had a lead singer named John Schlitt, whose worshipful heart and fabulous voice had been an inspiration to me. Sometimes I would stand in front of my mirror at home and sing along to my Petra cassettes, pretending that I was John Schlitt.

It was July, and the temperature had climbed to almost 100 degrees, so it got pretty overwhelming in the hot sun. But it was worth it. Where else could you go to hear this much live music that glorified God? And it rocked!

We mostly slept on top of our sleeping bags, all clustered around Sandy's van. It wasn't luxurious, but there was no place in the known universe I would rather have been. I had cash in my pocket from my job at the dairy farm, and I was free to spend it as I chose—on assorted deep-fried junk food, cassettes, or T-shirts and other swag from my favorite performers. I blew through most of my money on the first day.

Though I was undersized, and on my way to getting kind of chubby, I ate with abandon—elephant ears, corn dogs slathered with mustard, and all kinds of sweets. I was like "Ham" Porter from that movie *The Sandlot*. I never hesitated to stop and snatch a funnel cake. It wasn't healthy, but it was awesome. Clearly self-control was not one of the spiritual fruits that I'd attained. When my money ran low, I just took to eating whatever I could scrounge at our campsite.

I was in my element. And though the "cuisine" was great, I enjoyed the music and fellowship even more. We'd watch our favorite bands perform on stage and then gather around in lawn chairs at night to compare our notes and gossip about what we had seen and experienced.

I was sad when the last day rolled around, but also a little exhausted. In fact, everyone seemed to be losing energy and enthusiasm. Things were winding down, and people were starting to get a little cranky and irritable. Small squabbles broke out among the members of the youth group, and occasionally tempers would flare up. Most of the kids got lazy and didn't want to bother trying to get the best seats for the final show.

As the last show of the evening approached, I hung around the campsite until it was almost time for the show to begin. It was tempting to just skip it, but I meandered over to the place where they had opened the gates for the concert. When I got there, I noticed that there were still open spaces down front, and I made a beeline for them as fast as my short legs could carry me. When I got to the black metal security fence, I grabbed it and hung on for dear life. I had scored a prime location at the very front of the crowd, though I'll never understand how I managed it. I guess the crowds had miraculously parted like the sea did for the escaping Israelites fleeing Pharaoh's army.

After a few minutes, everything went dark and anticipation swept over the crowd. People roared with excitement, and camera flashes popped up all around. I was jammed up against the fence, but I felt the exhilaration all around me and was overcome with excitement myself.

Suddenly, a pulsing, ominous intro came slinking out of the darkness, and everyone erupted with applause and pandemonium. I felt a profound sensation of awe and wonder cascading through my body. The hair stood up on the back of my neck. I got goosebumps. Then the first words came from the darkened stage in time to the music "Down with the DC Talk, d-d, down with the DC Talk." Seconds later, the stage exploded with light, and there were dancers everywhere. And right in front of me, wildly rocking out to their song "Luv Is a Verb," was DC Talk.

They were so close I could almost touch them. I put my foot into one of the openings in the fence and hoisted myself up so I could look backward. Behind me were legions of people with their hands waving in the air and their bodies moving like rolling waves of the ocean, swaying from side to side.

It was pure celebration, wild abandon, and unadulterated joy.

And then something happened.

As the music built, something came awake within me, as though someone had shone a light into the dark, reclusive rooms of my heart. My feelings of inadequacy fell away, and I envisioned myself up on that stage, doing what they were doing: singing and testifying to the joy that they'd found in Jesus. Their message of hope slipped past every wall of self-protection I'd built around my heart, and with it came a spiritual presence that had arrived uninvited but was absolutely welcome and healing. I hung on to every word coming through their songs. The music moved my body, but the message moved my soul. I sang along to "Jesus Is Just Alright," "That Kinda Girl," and "Say the Words" as though I were a member of the band.

I didn't want the concert to end, but all too soon it did. This young man, walking back to his campsite, felt changed in ways that he couldn't really put into words. My eyes were brighter, and I was filled to the brim with hope and encouragement. I was soaring on a spiritual high. I knew something important had happened inside me during the concert.

The next morning we loaded the van and left the fairgrounds behind. Sitting in my seat in the van, I stared out the window and continued to imagine myself there on stage, singing with the band. I had a vision of TobyMac, founder and lead singer of DC Talk, passing me a baton, as though it were up to me to carry on the next portion of the race. It felt like this was Jesus' way of assuring me that He had plans for me...and that music would be central to these plans.

This vision stayed with me through the entire summer. It didn't feel like a dream as much as a destiny.

CHAPTER 6

A SEASON OF SHOCKS

Snapshot of me at about age 15:

I'm just over five feet tall, with pasty white skin, bright orange hair, and a face covered with freckles. I can barely stand to look at myself in the mirror. Sandy cuts my hair for free, but her talent in this area is limited, and usually my hair looks a little misshapen and weird. The accuracy of any haircut is always dependent upon how rushed she might be at that moment.

I'm still undersized and underdeveloped and still not happy about that. Perhaps as a compensation I have become a bit of a hellion. Because I am so small and mostly unable to defend myself physically against the bullies, I have found my defense in words and learned how to use them as weapons or as a way to fit in. I know how to get the upper hand with my "smart mouth," how to make an opponent back off in bewilderment, or how to get everyone laughing and thinking I am the cleverest guy around. Sometimes the combination of my way with words and my tendency toward a hot temper gets me into trouble.

I'm an adrenaline junkie and ready to throw caution to the wind. I help wrap toilet paper around the trees at a friend's house. I toss eggs at passing cars. I throw rotten food out the car window at other drivers. I go cliff diving from 40 feet into the raging Rogue River. I see how fast I can make a dirt bike go. I bungee jump. I party hard. And I outrun the police when caught in one of these activities.

And I feel a little guilt about all this because I am still trying to follow Jesus and be a good Christian. I don't want to disappoint or hurt my parents, who love me. I don't want to displease God either. I really don't want to hurt *anyone*. So in the midst of my rebellious phase I am trying to walk the fine line of being a good church boy and a rebel with (or without) a cause. My brazen thirst for adventure, my disrespect for authority, and my desire to please God are all mixed together. I have a desire to dance wildly around the fire, but I am hoping not to get burned.

To the stew of elements that made up my life at that age, I must, of course, add the one ingredient that affects every adolescent boy: desire for girls. But this longing was frustrated by my maddening inability to finish growing up physically. The other guys could catch the attention of the young ladies, but I had no such luck. Who would be interested in someone who looks like a freckled, flame-haired little boy? Coming out of junior high I prayed desperately that my hormones would kick in by the time I started high school.

However, when I started ninth grade my voice was still high pitched and I hadn't added a single inch to my height. I began to wonder if I would ever grow or if I would be stunted for life. The only growth I had managed was in my width. I was gaining weight and growing chubbier by the month.

One afternoon I was called to the nurse's office at school for a mandatory eye exam. I was nervous because I knew my vision wasn't very good. I had to squint to make out what was written on the board during class, and reading was a struggle. Sure enough, when the nurse asked me to read the chart I could do little more than make a good guess based on the general shapes of the letters. Needless to say, I failed the exam miserably. The nurse contacted my parents to let them know I needed glasses.

Glasses. Just great. As if I needed another obstacle to social acceptance. This was before anyone considered glasses to be cool, so I didn't want to have to wear them. When Mom took me to the optometrist I tried to figure out a way to beat the system by cheating about how well I could see. It didn't work. In fact, not only did the doctor confirm that I had a strong astigmatism, but he also discovered that I had a mild case of dyslexia and a severe case of color blindness. The latter is a rare kind that makes it difficult to distinguish between red and green. I remember that when he put color detection slides on the screen in front of me that suddenly I saw what everyone else was normally seeing. With those slides it seemed like I had some sort of visual superpower. And the moment they were removed, I was reminded of my visual inadequacies.

I tried on several pairs of glasses, trying to find one that didn't make me look like an old man or some character from *Revenge of the Nerds*. The only ones I really liked were way too expensive, so I had to settle for something that didn't really appeal to me.

Two weeks later, when the assistant fitted my brand-new glasses, she bent down in front of me, wrenching them into form. When she thought she had them right she looked me over and wasn't smiling. I think she knew that they didn't look very good, but of course she couldn't say so.

It wasn't much fun heading back to school with a fresh pair of glasses, especially when I'd never worn them before. Real or imagined, I interpreted every look, stare, snicker, or comment as a judgment upon my "new look," which was even less appealing than my "old look." In time I adjusted, and I've worn glasses ever since. But at the time it was just another thing to feel self-conscious about.

During the summer between my freshman and sophomore years my dad got a job working as a long-haul truck driver, delivering alfalfa to regional dairy farmers in a bright red semi with a trailer. One day he was returning from a trip to Chico, California, and heading home up the freeway. About the time he hit Cottonwood he noticed something large suddenly appear just ahead of him. As it turns out, it was a wheel and axle that had broken loose from a pickup traveling in the opposite direction. They came flying in his direction, tumbling across five lanes and barely missing several cars until they lodged under Dad's truck.

It all happened so fast he had no time to react. He slammed on the brakes, but it was to no avail. He lost control of the truck. It went careening off the road, eventually coming to a stop upside down on the right shoulder of the road. Dad was trapped inside and lost consciousness. The truck was crushed like it had gone through a compactor.

The state troopers from nearby Redding arrived on the scene, along with EMS and the fire department. They found Dad so tightly wedged into the wreckage that they couldn't free him without cutting the truck apart. It took nearly 50 minutes before he was extricated from the rubble. After they got him stabilized, they airlifted him by helicopter to Mercy Medical Center in Redding, where he spent the next ten days in the ICU. He had sustained bilateral compound fractures in both arms, which required the surgical placement of metal plates and screws in each of them. On top of that, he sustained a tension pneumothorax, a severe concussion, and various lacerations all over his body, many requiring extensive stitches and staples.

When we received the news about what had happened, my mom and sister were in Eugene, Oregon, investigating the possibility of Janay attending Lane Community College when Janay graduated high school the following fall. Miraculously, someone on campus was able to track them down and relay the news about the accident. They left what they were doing, jumped in the car, and raced home. They managed the normal three-and-a-half-hour trip in record time. I was working at the dairy that day, so Sandy let me know that Dad had been in a terrible accident. She told me that he was alive but in critical condition. So Sandy and I were waiting when Mom and Janay arrived, and Sandy took over the driving. We headed toward Redding as fast as we could go.

Entering the ICU room and seeing Dad, I nearly lost it. There he lay in that sterile white hospital room, his face almost unrecognizable thanks to the swelling and his skin purple and yellow from the extensive bruising. His eyes were glazed and puffy. Both arms were in casts, and the cast on his left arm went all the way up to his shoulder. He was hooked up to multiple IVs and had EKG electrodes all over his chest, an oxygen line attached to his nose, and a tube coming directly out of the side of his chest wall from between his ribs. I had to fight back tears and the fear that we might lose him.

He survived the night and slowly began an extended period of recovery.

In time Dad's health returned, though he was laid up for a long time. The healing was slow, but he took on occasional jobs as soon as he was able so that he could make some money to help build the family finances.

The medical bills were a nightmare. They piled up month after month, and our health insurance was totally insufficient. It didn't cover any accident involving uninsured drivers—and the fellow whose pickup axle came stalking across five lanes didn't have any insurance… or even a license. We were in a terrible spot, and the financial stress added to the pain my dad was still experiencing. It took years to get the family finances into order again.

Eventually Dad was healthy enough to work full-time again, and he got another job doing long-haul trucking. It was with a different company, and he mostly hauled lumber. But because we had come so close to losing him, I was on pins and needles every time he would pull out of the driveway. It made me angry, to be honest, and I wanted to forbid him to return to this kind of work. But there was little else he was qualified to do. My anger was mollified when he looked me in the eyes and said quietly, "This is all I can do."

Maybe this is the place for a few words about my wonderful sister, Janay. She is three years older than I am, so she was a senior the year I entered high school. It was fun attending school together for that one year, though it was always a race to see who could get home from school first. The issue was control of the television. If she got home first I'd find her in the recliner drinking a glass of iced tea and watching the soap opera *Days of Our Lives*. If, on the other hand, I arrived before her she would find me with a stack of chocolate chip cookies that Mom had hidden—not very successfully—in the freezer, along with a glass of milk. I would be tuned in to *Saved by the Bell*.

Our TV was an old Quasar with a pair of tinfoil-covered "bunny ear" antennas perched on top of it. It had a lot of quirks. We had to pull out the volume knob to turn it on, and to change the channel we had to turn the knob to choose which of the channels between 1 and 12 we wanted to watch. Honestly, though, we didn't even get 12 channels—only a couple local stations and TBS from Atlanta. (Since it was the "home of the Braves," I became a rabid fan of professional baseball and knew the whole lineup of Atlanta's team.)

Though Janay and I had different tastes in TV shows, we got along very well, and it was hard when she left home to go to college in Eugene.

With Dad on the road again in his truck and Janay off to Lane Community College, Mom and I found ourselves alone in the single-wide. It was pretty quiet, but it was a time when our relationship really grew and developed. At an age when many kids grow apart from their parents, Mom and I grew closer together. She trusted me, and I tried harder than before to be worthy of that trust. She also became like a second mom to my best friend, who had grown up with an abusive father and a mother who was seemingly never home. He was a latchkey kid who was woefully lacking in supervision. Mom stepped right into the gap. She adored Jed, and all three of us hung out regularly.

One May afternoon we were playing catch in the front yard when she returned from town. She pulled up in the driveway and walked right past me without saying a word. That was weird. She always stopped to see how I was doing or to tease me a little, but that day she had a really serious look on her face. A couple minutes later she called to me from the porch. "Ryan, can you come inside for a minute?" I was frustrated about being interrupted in my important business of doing nothing, but as I sat down on the couch beside her, she suddenly broke into tears.

She had just been diagnosed with stage four breast cancer.

Time stopped. I felt like Neo in *The Matrix*, when he held out his hand and everything came to a screeching halt in midair. I froze. The blood drained out of my face. I lost all sense of feeling in my body. And, as though someone had packed my ears full of cotton, I couldn't hear anything. I could see Mom's mouth moving as she explained, but I couldn't hear any words coming out.

Eventually I got the whole story. The doctors had discovered a malignant tumor in her left breast, and the cancer had already traveled to her lymph nodes—and from there it had taken the express route to the rest of her body. This came as a total surprise because she had always kept up to date on doctor visits and had a mammogram every two years like clockwork. On the last mammogram they hadn't found any problems.

They had to treat the cancer very aggressively. First, there was a mastectomy to remove her left breast. Then a lymphadenectomy to remove the lymph nodes under her left armpit and a hysterectomy to remove her ovaries and uterus. She also received a series of radiation treatments and chemotherapy infusions. Her hair began to fall out.

I remember one day Mom came into the living room clenching large clumps of hair in each hand and crying uncontrollably. She felt she was losing her womanhood and didn't want to watch her hair disappear in chunks. I decided it was time to give her a new look. We got the clippers from the bathroom, she took a seat in the kitchen on an old dining room chair, I draped a towel around her neck, and I gently shaved off her remaining hair. It was a tender moment between us that I will always cherish.

From then on, Mom was sick most of the time, and since no one else was around—Dad couldn't just quit his job—I became my mother's primary caretaker. I was the youngest, the baby of the family, her only son…and now I was her nurse. At times it was really uncomfortable, especially when she chose to confide in me about the personal issues she was dealing with. I was not only her nurse, but also her counselor. She'd confess how she was feeling, and it was almost more than I could take. She talked about how depressed she was, how she just wanted to die, how she couldn't stand the sight of herself because of her weight, and how appalled she was by her own appearance.

Then it got worse. She talked about how she felt that Dad no longer loved her and how poorly they communicated. She was constantly fearful that the family was going to lose everything because of our financial hardships. As a result of all this, a deep and debilitating depression descended upon her, along with a crippling sense of anxiety. Her emotional struggle affected me so deeply that the same feelings began to take hold within me. For both of us it felt like a test of fortitude…and of faith.

I wondered how much more bad news I could stand.

CHAPTER 7

CARS, SPORTS, AND GIRLS

When I got my driver's license it was more than just receiving legal permission to operate a vehicle. It was also a license for liberation. Suddenly I had the freedom to go wherever I wanted whenever I wanted. I didn't have to try to bum a ride or beg my parents to drop me off somewhere. The road was mine. Believe me, I embraced this freedom with both hands on the steering wheel.

The actual experience of getting my license was like something out of a comedy. Sandy and I were at the hospital with Mom, and we knew we had a long stretch of time before us in the waiting room. All of a sudden, Sandy put down the magazine she'd been flipping through and said, "Hey, why don't we go get your driver's license?"

That seemed like a great idea since the DMV was only a couple miles away. We could go there, and I could get the written test out of the way. That was really the only part of the process I was nervous about, since I'd already had a lot of actual time behind the wheel…at least out in the fields.

The test itself was on a computer, so I settled in front of the screen and got started. As I took the test, it gave me the results immediately. When I got the question right the word *correct* popped up, and whenever I made a mistake it would signal *incorrect* and then display the correct answer. As I neared the end of the test, I knew that my incorrect answers outweighed the correct ones. Clearly, I was going to fail.

Just then, however, there was an electrical failure and all the power went out in the building. The lights blinked off and the computer screen went blank. All the work I had done up to that part was gone and my score was erased. When power didn't return right away, the woman behind the counter had to dig up a paper version of the same test so I could finish. With pencil in hand I proceeded to ace the test. After all, the tests were identical, and now I knew the correct answers!

A week later I went back for the driving portion of the test and did just fine, even though I took the test in the family's 1981 Oldsmobile Cutlass Supreme—a big, ungainly vehicle that seemed to float across the asphalt like some sort of boat. The brakes were never dependable, but both the car and I managed to impress the guy from the DMV well enough to earn an 85 on the test. I was now a legal occupant of the open road, and I was ready to see where it would take me.

By my junior year I was even chunkier, but I still wasn't any taller. Everybody else was decked out with the latest styles in facial hair, but my face was as smooth as a baby's bottom. My natural athletic abilities began to fail me since I was now so undersized compared to the competition. There was no hope of getting a good position on the football team, so the best I could muster was to play center—the guy who hikes the ball to the quarterback. This meant that every play began with staring down some huge beast—a large, bulky, angry, and deranged defensive lineman. I was like a six-year-old trying to play against someone from the NFL. When I didn't prove very effective at defending the quarterback, I was left on the JV squad while just about everyone else moved up to varsity. I was so disappointed and humiliated that I tried to get that soccer coach who had once predicted great things for me to take me on the soccer team. He let me know that he wasn't interested.

So I did the only reasonable thing for a short, chubby guy to do—I went out for the basketball team. I was a midget in the land of the giants. I couldn't jump high enough to even touch the bottom of the net. The basketball coach had no patience with his players and doled out playing time based on some secret system of favoritism that I could never figure out. Then again, part of the problem was that my attitude stank. I was hotheaded, quick tempered, and not afraid to voice every complaint. No wonder I spent most of my time riding the bench.

My ego and my ambition were stronger than my sense of reality. There was always that inner voice whispering, "C'mon, Ryan, prove them all wrong. Don't quit. You can show them!" I should have just resigned myself to reality or learned to be satisfied with simply being part of the team, but my pride was too strong. So I kept finding new ways to humiliate myself.

It was a loooong year.

Finally, in the summer between my junior and senior years, whatever it was in my body that had not been getting the growth message suddenly kicked into gear. In just a few short months I grew from five foot two to five foot eight. My body became leaner and my muscles more defined. Hair began to sprout on my face and in other places. I was finally feeling like a young *man*, though there was a cost to my growth spurt, since my bones and joints seemed to be having a hard time accommodating the rapid maturation of my body. Especially my knees. Consequently, I was in pain most of the time. But I didn't care, as long as I was finally catching up with the rest of my class.

With these changes I finally found the confidence to pursue girls.

The best part of my senior year came in the form of a charming young lady named Sarah, who helped make the rest of the struggles in my life a little easier to bear. A tall, thin, blonde farm girl with blue eyes, she was just the kind of person I'd hoped to meet: athletic, very smart, quick witted, but generally quiet and tranquil. We met in geometry class when the teacher decided to pair up the kids who weren't getting it, like me, with students who were, like her. She became my classroom mentor, a freshman stuck trying to explain the finer points of mathematics to a clueless upperclassman. To break the tension of the situation, I fell back on my sense of humor. I made her laugh. Sometimes, when that didn't work, I would even sing a little song to her.

We started hanging out more regularly after we both volunteered to help with a cross-country bicycle event called Cycle Oregon, which brought hundreds of cyclists through our little town. We ended up working together the whole day, and by nightfall something had changed between us. I could tell by the fluttering of butterflies in the pit of my stomach that I had fallen for her—and, amazingly, she seemed to feel the same way.

I was too shy to ask her about our relationship to her face, so after hanging around together quite a lot for a few weeks, I picked up the phone, dialed her number, and managed to stammer out the words, "So, are you gonna be my girlfriend?"

"Are you ever gonna ask me?" she replied.

So I asked—officially—and she said yes. I had a girlfriend. I was in uncharted territory, but I loved it.

However, her dad decided she was too young to date, so we had to find tricky—and somewhat deceptive—ways to hang out. She would tell her parents that she was going to a movie "with friends," and then drive into town to meet me, her only actual "friend" for that evening. Our first real date involved a meal at McDonald's, which was the staple cuisine of every high school kid in Bonanza, then driving around with the windows down and singing along with songs from Third Eye Blind and Boyz II Men as loudly as we could, and finally topping off the evening with a movie at Pelican Cinema. In our eyes, we were the original Romeo and Juliet, so we watched the version starring Leonardo DiCaprio and Claire Danes, holding hands and cuddling in our seats. It was one of the most beautiful moments of my life up to that point.

Like so many first romances, ours was not destined to last. We started to rapidly cycle through breakups and reconciliations. Part of our problem was that I was so afraid of rejection that I'd push her away before she had a chance to reject me. Then I'd start missing her and want to get back together. Though we developed a real love for one another, we couldn't make a relationship work. She was sweet and accepting, but I was far too insecure to make something serious really take hold. Sarah and I remained close friends, and her presence in my life was a bright light in my sometimes dark inner reality. She was truly a gift.

After graduation I went back to work at the dairy and started saving up money for college.

CHAPTER 8

THE CROWD GOES WILD

Eugene, Oregon, sits in the heart of the Willamette Valley, tucked between two mountain ranges and only about an hour inland from the Oregon coast. The city gets quite a lot of rain, but the precipitation guarantees lush green surroundings. There are beautiful trees everywhere; fields with growing crops, rolling hills, and mountain views on both sides; as well as two rivers that flow through its heart on their way to the Pacific Ocean. It's a college town that sports a progressive, free-spirited vibe.

For someone raised in a conservative farming community, it took some adjustment to deal with the tie-dyed T-shirts, dreadlocks, hemp necklaces, bicycles, and vintage Volkswagen buses. Eugene is a hippie paradise, and I often detected the aroma of marijuana wafting through the air. The area even boasts a yearly country fair, which provides an opportunity to celebrate all kinds of alternative lifestyles, nudity, and general rebelliousness. As much as all this contrasted with my upbringing, there was still much for me to love about Eugene.

I'd considered a couple other options but decided that Eugene seemed like the best place to go to school. I figured I would probably attend the University of Oregon. Frankly, my parents were supportive of wherever I wanted to go. They were never going to be able to afford any of the options, so much of it came down to where I could put together the best financial aid package. Financially, I was on my own—and the $500 college scholarship I'd earned at high school wasn't going to go very far. It probably wouldn't even cover the cost of my books for the first term.

One afternoon my mother sat me down and told me about Northwest Christian College. I'd never even heard of it—a small Christian liberal arts college near the University of Oregon—but she'd heard great things from a friend whose son was attending there. Though initially resistant, I kept feeling a tug in that direction, so I finally said, "Let's go see it."

The very next morning we climbed into the Oldsmobile and drove three hours over the mountains to visit the school. I liked Eugene immediately and was impressed with the small college that fit snugly within a single city block. It was located right on the edge of the University of Oregon campus, a humble little beacon of light in a secular wasteland. The people from the school we sat down with were great, especially the admissions counselor, Scott, a friendly bleach-blond dude with spiked hair and a charismatic personality. He made me feel like this could be not just a school, but a home away from home. In the middle of our tour of the campus, he turned to me and gave me a serious look. "Dude," he exclaimed, "you totally need to be here. You should just apply now!" Then he flashed a smile.

Why not? I thought. *I can at least apply and see what happens.*

Well, Scott marched us right over to the admissions office and had me fill out some paperwork. He said he really wanted me to come, and he would try to see if I could get fast-tracked. He fiddled around with the application forms while Mom and I wandered around the campus, looking at the buildings and the landscape. I liked everything I saw. It all just felt so right, and I felt a sense of peace about being there.

After a short period of time I heard Scott calling out my name from across the courtyard. We ambled over to where he had emerged from the administration building, and he offered a smile and a big hug. "Dude," he said, "you're in!"

That was the end of my questions about college. This was the place I needed to be. So one week later I packed my stuff in my 1981 Subaru and moved to Eugene for my freshman year at NCC.

Music was about to become a major focus in my life. One of my graduation presents had been a guitar, given to me by my youth leader. One day he'd pulled up outside our trailer in his old beat-up truck and lifted an equally beat-up-looking guitar case from the front seat. "Here ya go. I just felt like the Lord told me I should give this to you."

When I opened the case, I discovered a brand new Samick acoustic guitar. I was appreciative, for sure, but wondered what he was thinking. After all, he knew that my passion was the drums. I'd been playing drums since I was in third grade, and I had become more than proficient. I was good. My dream was to someday be the drummer in a rock band. Of course, a drum kit is pretty expensive, and my family never had any extra money, so if I wanted to beat on anything other than Mom's pots and pans, I had to find some drums I could use. That meant that I mostly got my opportunity to play at school, either with the pep band or during band class.

I would have killed to have my own drum kit. Instead, here I was with a guitar. I wasn't even really interested in playing a guitar. So I thanked him for the gift and found a place for it in the back of my closet.

But that guitar was one of the things I hauled to Eugene with me when I took up residence in my little dorm room, which I shared with a guy named Dave. Dave was a stout Mexican kid from Medford, Oregon. He was full of energy and full of joy. He walked with a bit of a limp because he'd had his foot half torn off in an accident with his Jeep, but this really didn't slow him down very much. When we first met there was no formality to his greeting. He just nodded and said, "Hey, what's up?"

I loved the freedom of being on my own, and I could tell that the other guys in my dorm were breathing in that same intoxicating sense of liberation. It was a rush, and there was shared euphoria, especially since we had a few days without responsibilities before classes began. I began to make friends with the variety of guys who had been drawn to NCC along with me—a smorgasbord of athletes, preachers' kids, rebels, renegades, rejects, nerds, hippies, and wannabe musicians.

One of the things a lot of us had in common was that many of us owned guitars. It seemed like the dorm was filled with them. I decided that I might as well break mine out and fiddle around with it. Sitting on my bed one day, I held it out in front of me and gave it a good looking over. I had no idea what I was doing. I didn't know a single chord or strumming pattern. I just plucked some random strings to see how it would sound. Hmm... Not that great.

There was a knock on my door, and when I answered it I found myself standing face-to-face with a guy who could have been a *GQ* model. He had a look and manner that reminded me of Freddie Prinze Jr—tall, chiseled, and wreaking of self-confidence. I later learned that he had been a star athlete at his local high school and had earned a full-ride scholarship to play basketball for NCC. His name was Paul Wright.

A free spirit who oozed charisma, Paul had a contagious sense of charm. He plopped down on the bed across from me and sized up my guitar. I had to admit that I had no idea how to play it. He got up and left the room without a word, only to return a minute later with his own guitar. Sitting across from me, he showed me some simple chords. I watched where he put his fingers and how he strummed, and I started to mimic his movements. It took almost no time at all before I started sounding like I knew what I was doing.

Somehow it seemed as though the guitar and I had been destined for each other, even though I had never given any serious thought to being a guitarist. Soon Paul and I were jamming together. I played the rhythm part, and he filled in with some beautiful melodies. The resulting sound was magical. A special bond was born that day, and I discovered the instrument and a friendship that would be so important to my future.

As my skills developed and our friendship grew, Paul and I began to hang out all the time and make music. He was a rapper, with an incredible ability to freestyle. Like him, I was totally into hip-hop, and my background with drums created a rhythmic dynamic between us that was flawless. As I learned the strumming techniques I needed to create a pop sound, he would sometimes freestyle over my acoustic progressions. I didn't have much confidence in my singing ability, but I learned how to double him on the choruses. Our voices blended beautifully. Sometimes we'd finish a song and just stare at each other in amazement at what had just happened.

We were making music. Good music.

Our two voices and two guitars created a distinctive sound, and we worked on developing it. Often we'd completely lose track of time as we became more and more immersed in what we were coming to recognize as our newly formed "group." We became more intentional about writing songs together—actual, bona fide songs with verses, choruses, bridges, and dope melodic hooks. It was awesome.

A lot of our songs featured the typical teenage fare of summer, girls, and good times. But because we were both serious about our faith, we managed to infuse Jesus into all the songs. When Paul was supposed to be paying attention to a lecture on English literature or the Bible, he was often writing lyrics for our songs. After classes we'd retreat to my room and get out our guitars, and he'd show me what he had created during Old Testament Survey. I'd start playing along with some chords, vocally inserting some melodies, and it would all seamlessly fit with what he'd been working on. It felt as though these had always been songs and they were just waiting for us to discover them and make them real.

JC Cross was the name we gave our band when we decided we wanted to share this music with others. It was a name carried over from Paul's former rap trio in high school, but since the days of white-boy gangsta rap were over, our little acoustic duo assumed the name. I'd never performed music in front of anyone, and the thought of it was petrifying, but Paul's unshakable confidence convinced me that we could do it.

Without telling me, he signed us up to perform at an open mic night at Cafe Paradiso in downtown Eugene, a little coffee shop that seated maybe 50 people. This would be our first public performance. Since word had spread around campus that Paul and I were making some awesome music, bunches of our fellow students showed up for our musical debut. They packed in, more than 100 students sitting at tables or on the floor or standing in the back. A few even found a place to perch on the edge of the stage. People were crammed shoulder to shoulder, and because everyone was jammed in so tightly—all the way back to the door—there wasn't room for the regular patrons to get in.

When our turn came, Paul and I took the stage and rocked the house for our allotted ten minutes, playing extended versions of only two songs. Our rhythmic strumming, fresh and funky pop chords, smooth harmonies, and my beatbox beneath Paul's rapping combined to make a sound that drove the crowd wild. We had the audience in the palm of our hands, and no one wanted us to stop. They begged to hear more, but the owner had to let the next scheduled band have their turn.

As we packed up our instruments, the proprietor literally begged us to come back and play. He loved the turnout, and we were obviously good for business. I felt bad for the next act. As we left, the place quickly emptied behind us.

JC Cross had left the building.

CHAPTER 9

A MOMENT OF GLORY, DAYS OF PAIN

Our musical success all happened fast, and it was a glorious ride while it lasted. After our coffee house gig, it seemed like there was no stopping us.

We began to get more invitations to play, and our vibe just got stronger and tighter. We knew that we could make great music together, and we did at every available opportunity. If we weren't in class or playing basketball, we were either practicing or playing somewhere—coffeehouses, camps, churches, youth groups, high schools, or even other colleges. We rarely turned down an opportunity to rock the house with our blend of hip-hop, funk, and acoustic pop.

Two years in, we decided that something was missing, so we added a bass player and a drummer. At this point we figured we ought to celebrate this next step with a new band name, so we christened ourselves Front Row Joe. Don't ask me what that meant; it just sounded cool.

We'd sequester ourselves in the NCC chapel every Thursday night and rehearse our set, which just kept getting tighter. We were now playing all over the place, and Paul's beeper was always going off. The size of the concerts grew, and we began to land significant festival shows like Creation Fest, which had become the Jesus Northwest of that day and drew people from all over the Pacific Northwest for a megafestival with all the hottest Christian music acts.

When I wasn't playing with Front Row Joe, I was backing up the worship band at my church led by Ken Brown. Ken became one of my dearest friends and confidants. And when the time came he was also the guy I asked to marry my wife and me. But that's getting ahead of my story.

The band manager for Front Row Joe was a guy named DJ. He wasn't a professional manager, but he still managed to get us some good gigs. One morning during my senior year he called to let me know that a local promoter had approached him about having our band open for Switchfoot at the McDonald Theater downtown the following weekend. At the time, this was the best venue in Eugene, and Switchfoot was at the height of their fame, getting general market attention and performing sold-out shows all over the world. They had just contributed to the soundtrack for the Mandy Moore movie, *A Walk to Remember*, and their song "Dare You to Move" had just debuted.

Of course, there wasn't even the slightest hesitation on our part about saying yes, even if it meant having to go find some suitable clothes to wear for the performance. My budget was still very limited, so I bought an American flag shirt from Walmart and a pair of red cutoff sweatpants from Goodwill, and I finished off the look with a red bandanna around my head. I was ready!

That weekend we found ourselves hanging out backstage with one of the hottest bands in the world, and honestly…I felt pretty nervous. But the guys from Switchfoot were super cool and treated us with a lot of respect. Before long we heard the dampened roar of fans flooding into the theater. I got chills up the back of my neck. Then the fire marshal came into the green room and let us know that the venue had reached maximum legal capacity—1,600 people. Because of the fire code, about 800 fans had to be turned away. This was the big time.

Just a couple minutes before the start time we all huddled up and prayed for the concert to be a blessing to everyone who attended. Then we moved to the wings to await our introduction from the MC.

As we took the stage in the dark I plugged in my guitar and strummed the first notes. The lights came up, and I was unprepared for what I saw. The audience was crammed into the building right up to the foot of the stage, and they were wild and sweaty and ready to go.

Honestly, for a few minutes it didn't even feel real. The energy in the room was insane. There wasn't one person in their seat. Everyone was on their feet and screaming.

For 30 minutes we rocked the house. We played our hearts out with the audience pushing us forward to one of the best performances we'd ever given. We left everything we had out on the stage, and it was pure euphoria. After our set Switchfoot took the stage, and we gathered in the wings, feeling giddy with energy and excitement. It was like we had just ascended Mount Everest and danced at the very peak. We all believed that show was an important milestone for our developing band and a sign of what the future would hold for us.

I was a big fan of Switchfoot, so while they were playing I decided to sneak into the auditorium and catch some of their performance. But a bunch of fans recognized me and went a little crazy, grabbing at my Walmart shirt, not believing that I had joined them in the audience. When I finally found a safe place from which to watch the show, I stood there in the reflected light, my heart full and a sparkle in my eyes. Jon Foreman and Switchfoot put on an amazing show, and I felt grateful and proud that we'd been a part of it.

After the show Switchfoot was full of praise for our performance—except for their road manager, who was a little ticked that our drummer had gotten so worked up while keeping the beat that he had literally busted a hole in their snare drum! But the band, including their drummer, was pretty cool about the whole thing.

It seemed like the time was right to record a professional demo, so we went into the studio with a local producer named Chris. We'd made our own demos up to this point, and to us they sounded awesome. But it was time for something more professional, with all the bells and whistles of a polished production. Over the course of a week or two we created a five-song EP in Chris' studio. If we were going to be a serious band we needed an album, and we were happy to have something to offer for sale at our shows.

For Paul, Front Row Joe was only one piece of his whole musical vision. So while our band was developing he was also doing some solo shows and collaborating with other local musicians. He was a great writer and needed more outlets than just our four-piece band. Over the years Paul had filled one notebook after another with song ideas and finished numbers. As much as he loved our band and wanted to see it attain great success, he still had a desire to release his own songs in his own distinct way. He had been at it for a lot longer than I had, and his ambition outpaced my own.

When I graduated from college I moved back to Bonanza to get a job, and our bass player moved home to Washington. I think we all started to feel a bit of uncertainty about what would become of our band, and we were still a long way from being able to make any kind of living from our music. But despite the distance between the members of the group I was still fully committed to the future of Front Row Joe. Paul, on the other hand, decided that the questionable status of our future together meant that he should double down on his pursuit of a solo career.

He started to share the EP we'd created with some movers and shakers in the Christian music business, along with a bunch of new demos he'd been recording on the side. It wasn't long before a batch of Paul's songs made their way into the hands of a rep at Gotee Records in Nashville, Tennessee, a label cofounded by the legendary TobyMac of DC Talk.

One weekend I was back in Eugene and staying at Paul's house, where he lived with his mom and stepdad. We were sitting around the kitchen table eating hummus and chips when he paused, took a deep breath, and got a funny sort of look on his face. He was quiet for a moment and then delivered his surprising news: He'd been offered a record deal with Gotee Records.

I was instantly over the moon with excitement, assuming this meant our band would finally get our chance at the big time. This would be the doorway into a full-time ministry of music.

Paul hesitated, a chip poised in midair, and quietly informed me that this wasn't about the band. It was a contract for him, not for Front Row Joe. He was being given an opportunity, and he felt like he needed to go in a different direction, so he was going to focus on making a record as a solo artist.

My heart sank.

It felt like my dreams had just risen from the table and walked out the door. I didn't know how to respond. I was hurt and angry and confused. *How could he do this?* Right then and there, those old voices of rejection and insecurity that I had heard since childhood came roaring back. My gut clenched and I wanted to cry, to plead and beg him to reconsider. I wanted to scream aloud about my feelings of betrayal. Instead, I gathered my composure, told him I was excited for him, got into my Subaru, and drove back to Bonanza, feeling weak and sick in my gut. I was shaking. I cried most of the way home.

I struggled for months with how to absorb this information. After all, he was one of my very best friends and a dear brother. We'd spent the last four years building something special together. I was angry; I was hurt; I felt betrayed. But I still loved him. And I was happy for him. I truly was. He had worked toward this goal for a lot longer than the time I'd known him, and now he was getting his chance. I just wished I was going along for the ride.

It got even harder during the next several months as his solo career began to take shape and blossom. I had to battle the feelings of resentment and disillusionment that were growing within me. It wasn't fair. I became bitter. When I heard one of his songs on the radio one day, I could barely stand to listen to it. I couldn't help but wish that the two of us where singing together on the radio.

It felt like I had just wasted the last four years of my life, and I wondered if God had something in store for me other than music.

Maybe I just needed a real job and a normal life.

CHAPTER 10

TRUE LOVE WAITS... AND WAITS

Rejection is a strange thing. It works insidiously, like a river carving its way through the landscape by slowly eating away at everything in its path. The river of rejection had created a Grand Canyon of insecurity in my heart, and it had all started with the trickling stream of self-pity, which had slowly and almost unnoticeably carved a monstrous gorge through the center of my self-confidence.

While I had been chasing the musical dream, I had also started chasing girls—in my own tentative way. I guess I should say I was *wanting* to chase girls. But I had to overcome my relational inexperience and the mockery I'd received from members of the opposite sex during my high school years. I'd only had the one romantic attachment in high school, and it had ended with more of a whimper than a bang.

I could check off all the boxes in my favor. I was…

- single
- reasonably good looking
- talented
- somewhat athletic (even though my late growth spurt had played havoc with my coordination)
- a basically good guy

But I still couldn't seem to figure out how to feel confident around girls. And now that I was an adult and on my own, a good relationship with a sweet young lady seemed like the next important thing I needed in my life.

I wasn't looking for sex as much as I was looking for someone who would care about me and I could care about them. I'd been raised with the discipline of sexual purity and the conviction that I should wait to have sex until marriage. Honestly, though, I was afraid to have sex anyway. And looking back, I know I wasn't ready at all for the kind of relationship I really wanted.

On the other hand, I'd heard all the stories, even from members of youth group, about various sexual escapades. These young men basked proudly in the glory of their accomplishments and prowess and the *amazing* sex they had experienced. Looking back, I realize that many of their stories were probably wishful fictions, but at the time it seemed like I was missing out on something. So I bought into the idea that as long as I didn't have actual intercourse with a girl, I could fool around pretty aggressively and push the limits right up to that line. After all, if I didn't have actual sex I was still a virgin, and that was the main thing, right?

Of course, I knew that I was believing this lie because it was what I wanted to believe, and because I was worried that maybe I was missing out on something perfectly natural because I was too concerned about sexual purity. If purity was a matter of heart, then I honestly wasn't very pure at all. I wasn't having wild and abandoned sex yet, but I was stewing in my own lust. And eventually that lust took me to a place I hadn't initially intended to go.

Tampering with lust is like taking a nibble at forbidden fruit. It looks like exactly what you want—something alluring and mysterious and desirable—and it gives the impression that a single bite will bring total fulfillment. Like heroin, though, even just one dose can get you hooked. That first high doesn't last, and it leaves you craving more. You never are sated.

My own personal "heroin" was being desired by girls, and soon I got to the point where I'd go to almost any length to get my fix. I wanted to be wanted. Once I was, though, I'd quickly tire of the relationship and would be ready to move on. It was a sick cycle. I bounced from one girl to the next in constant pursuit of the next thrill.

Even though I wasn't engaging in actual intercourse, I still believed that being physically involved would give me worth. After all, wasn't everyone doing it? Didn't it make me a real man? I thought I was Alexander the Great, conquering the world one girl at a time and staking my flag in the ground as proof of my conquest.

The problem was that many of the girls seemed to feel the same way, that fooling around was something that proved they were loved and desired and accepted. It wasn't hard to find a girl who wanted exactly what I wanted—or at least what I *thought* I wanted.

But after every encounter the momentary high was followed by a crushing sense of guilt. I was disgusted with myself. I felt like I was slowly being buried under a load of shame. Who was I fooling? My choices weren't about love. They were about a deep selfishness and a lack of self-control, honor, and respect. This cycle went against everything I believed in. I found myself trapped in a web of temporary and random relationships, where I gave and received what I thought was true commitment. It wasn't. It was just a way to wrestle with my deep sense of inadequacy. But nothing I was doing helped at all with that core problem.

Then I turned 21 and had legal access to alcohol, which was like turning up the temperature under the pressure cooker. I dove headfirst into a life of drinking, partying, and not getting enough sleep. I was often sick, in a daze, and totally exhausted. Then, come Sunday morning, I would stand on the stage with the worship band and help lead people in praising Jesus.

It was disgraceful, and I felt like a poser for living a double life. My conscience bothered me, but I was in too deep and didn't know how to change. I refused to accept that I had a problem as my routine of partying and drinking spiraled out of control. I told myself that this was just part of the phase that college guys go through.

I'm lucky I didn't end up dead. Believe me, there were some close calls.

One night a few of my buddies and I drove 50 miles up the twisting, winding, and heavily wooded McKenzie River Highway for an engagement party at a bar. We all proceeded to get wasted, and the bartender singled me out in particular and told my buddies, "He's cut off." The bartender was right to call me out. I was so inebriated that I tried to go number two in the urinal. When the bouncer found me laughing uproariously and perched upon the urinal doing my business, he flipped out. We were all kicked out of the bar.

Somehow, I made it to the back seat of my friend's car. All I know is that I hadn't been able to get there on my own. Since one of us was a little less drunk than the rest, the guy who owned the car was given the keys. It was a terrifying drive home. My roommate and I were semi-incoherent in the backseat, and we tried munching on an old box of Triscuits we found on the floor. All this accomplished was to make us both vomit repeatedly out the car windows all the way home.

The driver did his best to stay in his own lane on the winding roads, but our vehicle kept wandering into the oncoming lane, where it was met with the blasting horns of log trucks roaring home on their late-night runs. As I saw their lights coming toward us, I was convinced that I was going to die that very night. It seems a miracle that I didn't.

I woke up the next day in a parking garage in Eugene underneath someone else's car, with alcohol poisoning and little recollection of the events of the night before. It was all just a blur.

But did I learn my lesson? Not at all. I was ready for another such "adventure" at the nearest opportunity. Through undeserved grace, though, God seemed to be looking out for me, even as I strayed from what I believed. Through it all, He still loved this reckless prodigal. He was with me even there—in the center of my self-inflicted storm of craziness.

In the middle of all this craziness came an encounter that would change my life forever.

I had just finished my lunch in the NCC cafeteria, and as I stood up to leave someone bumped into me with a full tray of food, which spilled everywhere…including on me. When I turned to see the culprit, I found a gorgeous, well-tanned girl with a semi-panicked and sheepish look on her face. The entire room had heard the clatter of silverware and seen the splatter of various kinds of food and the drinking glass still spinning on the floor amid the debris.

She was frozen. Not by my charm, but by her embarrassment. "I'm so sorry, I'm so sorry, I'm so sorry," were the only words she could manage to put together as everyone's eyes locked onto the noisy mishap.

I wasn't the least bit bothered. In fact, I thought it was funny. The girl grabbed the tray, and I helped her scoop up the remnants of food. Before I could say anything to her, she just disappeared. I didn't even see her go. She simply vanished, not even staying to refill her plate. *Hmmm*, I thought to myself, *she's cute*.

Later that same day I went shopping at the local mall, Valley River Center. My usual plan, just as soon as I got my work-study check, was to blow most of my earnings on shoes and clothes. I was browsing through a rack at the Gap when I saw someone peering through the other side. Caught like a deer in the headlights was the girl I had collided with just hours before.

She seemed a little embarrassed but not at all unhappy to see me. She apologized again and then flashed a totally winning smile. We made a little small talk, and I discovered that she had a wonderful personality to go with her fabulous looks. When we parted, I smiled at my discovery. She was kind of awesome.

Then, a few hours later, I planned to join a friend at a coffee shop on Thirteenth Avenue. I walked in the front door and scoped out the place. Guess who was there? The same girl, sitting on the hearth of the fireplace. *This is weird*, I thought. But I didn't hesitate to go over and sit down beside her.

Her name was Kimberly Thomas, and we spent the next couple hours neglecting our friends and having a long conversation. As we walked back to campus together, we talked some more, and then we sat in the lounge of the dorm and kept talking. The more we talked, the more convinced I was that she was someone special, unlike any other girl I'd met. She was calm and sure of herself. She wasn't needy, clingy, or dramatic. In other words, she was the exact opposite of my personality, and I loved that.

Within a week we were officially a couple, and for the first time it felt like I was in an adult relationship—not with a girl, but with a woman. She felt like a safe person, and I knew that I could be myself around her—my true self, not the reckless and insecure idiot I had recently become.

Kim had been born and raised in Boise, Idaho, and was the oldest child in her family, which accounted for her steadiness and sense of responsibility. She came from a family that liked to hunt and fish and go camping. She loved nature, cooking, and homemaking. Since I was a country boy at heart, this meant we loved a lot of the same things. We started spending a lot of time together: seeing movies, shopping, or just engaging in long and deep conversations about the things that mattered to us. The more time we spent together, the more comfortable we felt with each other. Since neither of us had ever really had a significant romantic relationship as adults, we felt like we were each other's clean slate.

In her presence I regretted the lifestyle I'd been living. I was ready for a change.

But my old emotional issues weren't totally behind me. The feelings of shame and rejection caused me to hold back, smothering me like a swarm of hornets. I wasn't prepared to offer her any promise of a future together due to my commitment phobia. She was ready to take me on "as is," with all my quirks and imperfections, but I held back. I was afraid of being hurt if things didn't work out, so I undermined the relationship.

We underwent a series of breakups and reconnections, all of which were my fault. I'd break up with her, feel a bit of freedom, start to feel bad and miss her company, and then beg for her to take me back. It was just crazy. For some reason she was always willing to take me back.

While we were in a period of being "broken up" I would sometimes slide back into my old habits and chase any attractive girl who was handy. During one of our breakups Kim came unannounced to visit my apartment and found me there with another girl. She caught me with the lights low and some sexy R&B songs playing on the CD player. Knowing immediately what I was up to, she turned in the doorway and left without a word.

I didn't think it was a big deal, and honestly, I just assumed we'd get back together. We always did. But this time was different. When I knocked on the door of her apartment later on after the girl had left, Kim was crying, and between the tears came these words in a defiant tone: "Leave me alone. Don't call me. I never want to see you again. I'm done."

I was a little sorry, but I brushed it off and thought she was "just being emotional." Things would blow over.

But they didn't.

She *was* done with me. She wouldn't answer phone calls or open the door when I knocked. The more I tried to contact her, the more she dug in her heels. She became distant, and I finally awakened to how messed up I really was. She was the one person I could really be open with, but now I had lost her. I felt lonely and desperate.

I spent hours crying, praying, and reading the Bible. I was hoping for a miracle. I wasn't sleeping well or eating very much, and I felt nauseous most of the time. I took long walks beside the river and wallowed in my pain. I felt completely lost without her and sank deeper into depression.

I kept calling. But as weeks went by she still refused to talk with me. All my calls went directly to voicemail and she never called back. I sank deeper into depression and desperation. Now that I understood that I had probably lost Kim forever, I fully realized how much I wanted and needed her. I began to realize as never before how much I was trapped by my insecurities and my feelings of inadequacy. I understood for the first time that I was a broken person who needed healing, and that realization was the first step to letting the healing begin.

One day I summoned up my courage for what I determined would be one last effort to communicate with her. I rehearsed in my mind a somber message of goodbye, which I was prepared to leave on her voice mail. I punched in her number and listened to the phone ring on her end. To my amazement, she picked up. I was so surprised to hear her actual voice that it took me a few seconds to figure out what to say. Her opening line was simply, "What?"

I took a deep breath and asked her if we could meet face-to-face so I could apologize. I begged her to let me look into her eyes and tell her I was sorry. "You don't owe me anything, and you have every right to say no," I told her. "But please…"

To my astonishment, she said yes. She said she would come to my apartment, but she wouldn't come inside, and she wouldn't stay for more than a few minutes.

I had no great expectation, but I did feel a little spark of hope ignite inside me. I watched from the window, and when I saw her car pull up, I started to get nervous. As she got out of the car, her body language told me that she was in a cautious mood and her guard was up. She had, of course, built a mile-high wall around her heart, and clearly nothing I could say would penetrate. I rushed outside and met her on the little bench beside the building.

When I opened my mouth to speak, all I could get out was, "Kim, I'm just so sorry. I have no excuses," before the tears sprung to my eyes and I started crying. I tried to express what a fool I had been, how I had wronged her, and how much she meant to me. I told her that I recognized how dysfunctional I was, how ashamed I was for betraying her trust, and how much I regretted dragging her through all my immature stupidity. The whole conversation—well, it was more like a monologue—lasted about ten minutes. When my tearful confession finally came to an end, I looked her straight in the eye and said it one more time: "I'm sorry."

"Okay. Thanks," was her only response. She got back in her car, started the engine, shifted into drive, and pulled away. As her car disappeared into the distance, I knew that it was over, that my last glimmer of hope was gone. I had laid my cards on the table and my heart on the line, and she had barely responded. Not the slightest evidence of emotion.

Twenty minutes later, my phone rang.

It was Kim, and though her tone was still guarded, she invited me over for dinner. I got into my car and raced to her place. As I was driving there I tried to make sense of what was happening, and once again a glimmer of hope started to rise within me. Might there still be some future for the two of us after all? Still, I knew that I wasn't off the hook. I was like the rodent who was cautiously trying to sniff his way back to a crumb that he had forgotten on the floor.

When I arrived, I found that she had started cooking a gourmet meal for the two of us. I took a seat in her recliner as she stood in the kitchen, stirring some veggies in a skillet. Suddenly, she stopped, pushed the skillet off the burner, walked into the living room, and sat down on my lap. Looking into my confused and still bloodshot eyes, she didn't say a word. She just put her head against my neck, snuggling in close. There were no words from either of us, just deep sighs of relief, comfort, and hope. I felt like I had been enveloped in a supernatural sense of peace and calm, engulfed as though in a warm blanket.

It was clear to me in that moment that Kim was absolutely the only woman I had ever wanted and the only woman I would ever want. I wanted to commit my life to her and only her.

I was ready for a real and permanent change.

After that evening we were rarely apart. Her patience and discernment had broken through all my walls of self-protection and insecurity. She held the key that unlocked me and set me free.

A couple weeks later I bought an engagement ring. Before I proposed, I called her dad and asked for her hand in marriage. He seemed a little apprehensive—perhaps he had heard the stories—but he grudgingly gave his okay anyway. It must not have been easy for her parents to give their beloved daughter away to some lower-class kid from Bonanza, Oregon, who had bleach-blond hair, ear piercings, a tongue ring, and some failed dreams of rock and roll, but they were kind enough to say yes.

On January 9, 2002, Kim and I took a walk along the banks of the Willamette River. I brought along my guitar and the engagement ring. There, on some concrete steps leading down to the river, and with Autzen Stadium looming in the background, I played her a little song I had written especially for her. When the last note died away, I knelt in front of her, pulled the ring from my pocket, and asked her in a quivering voice if she would marry me. Tears sprung to her eyes and she said simply, "Yes."

Then came the job of planning the wedding and figuring out how we would survive financially once we had tied the knot. We believed with everything inside us that we would make it work.

The wedding took place in August 2002 in Boise, Idaho, in the backyard of Kim's grandparents' home. We were surrounded by our friends and families, and my pastor friend, Ken, performed the ceremony. Richard was my best man, and alongside him stood Willem, Jed, and Paul, as well as my brother-in-law, Kelly. It wasn't a fancy wedding. We'd managed to put it together on a very limited budget, and the food was provided by a potluck put together by Kim's mom and her friends. We filled an old rusted wheelbarrow with ice and Coronas. Nothing about the wedding was extravagant, but for us, it was perfect.

We planned to spend the first night of our honeymoon at a nice hotel down by the Boise River. We were so exhausted and hungry after the wedding that we stopped on our way to pick up something to eat at Taco Bell. I can imagine how we looked as we pulled up at the drive-through wearing a tuxedo and a wedding dress. Definitely high-class diners!

The next morning, we drove to Rockaway Beach, Oregon, where we enjoyed the two days we could afford at a hotel on the Oregon coast. We had a great time, and I loved introducing her to everyone we met as my wife, Kim Stevenson.

And then it was back to Bonanza to start our new life together.

CHAPTER 11

TEACHER AND STUDENT

I graduated with a bachelor's degree in elementary education, so it only made sense to look for a teaching job. I had entered college with the plan of pursuing a pre-med program, and I'd applied to study biology at the University of Oregon at the same time as I took my other classes at Northwest Christian College. My admissions counselor had recommended this path, but it soon proved to be a bad decision.

With all my focus on music during my early days of college I didn't ever seem to find the time to study the way I should. In fact, by the end of my first term I was on academic probation. Too much music and too little studying spelled trouble. When it came time to declare a major I thought through my options and realized that all I really cared about was getting through college in four years and emerging with a degree. I didn't want the student loan money to go to waste. At the time I planned to pursue my natural path of making music. I figured that a degree in education would be the path of least resistance to getting that diploma with my name on it.

By the time I was done with school I'd given up any hope of making real money in music. My dreams had died with Paul's solo success. So after graduation I decided to put my teaching degree to work, and I got a job teaching a morning kindergarten class and overseeing the after-school program.

I actually had a lot of fun during that year of teaching kindergarten, and it was so fulfilling to help those little turkeys learn to read and write. At their young age there wasn't a lot of pressure toward academic excellence, so I found it easy and fun to guide them along the path to learning. I think they enjoyed the fact that I usually taught with a guitar in my hands, using music and songs to give them the basic information they needed. I composed some great little ditties about reading and simple arithmetic, if I do say so myself! I probably had as much fun as they did.

The next year wasn't so fun. I was hired by a private Christian school and made the whopping sum of $580 every two weeks. Private schools like this one never paid well, and a good number of the students were clearly there against their will. Kids mostly attended a Christian school like this because their parents were wealthy and could afford to shelter their children in a safe little Christian bubble (protecting them from the real world—even if their kids would rather go to the local public school) or because they had been troublemakers who got kicked out of public school and were being sent to a private school to "straighten them out." In either case, whether privileged or troubled, most of them weren't happy to be there and seemed bent on making my job as difficult as possible.

My position was that of "utility" teacher, meaning I was a catch-all, a jack of all trades who got stuck with the subjects no one else really wanted to teach. Therefore, I found myself, still only a year out of college myself, teaching seventh-grade math, eighth-grade health, ninth-grade English, tenth-grade introductory Spanish, eleventh-grade Spanish, PE, and choir. On top of that I was made the assistant track coach.

When I had been interviewed for the job this all sounded like an amazing opportunity, but as the year began I immediately started to drown in a sea of lesson planning, grading, report cards, and dealing with a lot of bad attitudes from the students. Even with my education degree I felt like a fish out of water, gasping for breath, with no clue about how to survive the situation.

I was only 23 years old, and some of my students were as old as 18. Many of them were kids I had grown up around, so I had known them their whole life. It felt weird to have them call me "Mr. Stevenson," and it was even weirder when it came time for parent-teacher conferences.

Honestly, I felt like I was on trial for each child's educational failures. It was uncomfortable and embarrassing, and it didn't take long for me to realize that I wasn't a very effective teacher. After all, you can't teach advanced math or health science with a guitar. My best teaching methods from the kindergarten classes wouldn't work here. I was a joke as a teacher, and my students had my number. I was walking on eggshells, so they smelled blood in the water and ate me alive.

Needless to say, my teaching career only lasted through that year. When the end of the school year arrived, they were ready to see me leave, and I was more than ready to go. I had been excited about the idea of integrating a real love for Jesus with the process of learning, but instead found myself immersed in a world of hypocrisy, greed, and manipulation. The whole environment was so toxic, with unfair and ineffective administrative politics and resentful and unruly students, that several other teachers left the same year I did. While it was still true that I wasn't a very good teacher, the multiple defections at least confirmed I wasn't just crazy.

By the end of the year my self-esteem had been flattened by a fast-moving Mack truck. I had the psychological tread marks to prove it. To be honest, I'm just glad I survived without a mental breakdown.

And to top it all off, I discovered that I really didn't have the right set of gifts to be a good teacher. I had my degree, but it was clear that this wasn't a good direction for my life.

So what next? I thought that maybe Kim and I could just settle down in Bonanza and I could get a job with a local farmer or rancher. It was something I knew how to do, and it could help make ends meet. But it wasn't what I really wanted to do. Kim, at the same time, had a job for a while at a bank in Klamath Falls, but it was high stress and she was miserable. I wanted to make enough money so she wouldn't have to struggle along at a job she hated.

My old thoughts about a career in the medical field started to nag at me again. I couldn't find any programs at the local college that seemed exactly right. Plus, we certainly didn't have the money for me to go to medical school for six years. I'd already had just about enough of school anyway.

What to do?

Then Kim's mom called from Idaho one afternoon as we were driving home from our jobs. She wanted to let us know that Kim's grandparents were really struggling. Her grandfather had developed a severe lung disease that was terminal, and her grandmother had slipped into full-blown Alzheimer's and couldn't take care of him—or even herself. Kim's mom had been working around the clock and trying to do as much for them as she could, but it was starting to take a toll on her. There was no one else in the family who had the time or resources to help, and it looked like it would be necessary to place Kim's grandparents in an assisted living facility.

Kim was anxious about having to do that, feeling like she was letting her grandparents down.

As I heard the conversation, I felt a strong nudge from God. It was a calm and peaceful voice calling me to do something a little bit crazy: "You need to move to Idaho."

I had never wanted to live in Idaho. Oregon was home, and I figured it always would be. In fact, I'd told Kim that one condition for getting married was that she'd promise we would never move to Idaho. Frankly, there had been no argument; she didn't want to live in Idaho either. So this was a rock-solid agreement between us. That's why she was shocked when I blurted out, "We need to move to Idaho!"

The words just came out, and I was unable to catch them before it was too late. I suppose I looked like a little kid who had just let a naughty word slip and then covered his mouth in embarrassment about what he had just said. Kim, who was driving, looked at me like I was insane and nearly swerved off the road in confusion. But I knew in my heart that it was the right decision. So I said it again.

We needed to move to Idaho and help her grandparents. Why should the family put them in a care facility when we could care for them? What was there to hold us back? And hadn't God whispered it clearly into my heart that we ought to do this? Her grandfather was initially unsure about having us move in, but he soon realized this was the answer to many of their struggles.

Five days after that phone call, just one day before our first anniversary, we packed up what little we had in our rickety old Ford Explorer and moved to Boise. We didn't know what to expect, but we were confident we were doing the right thing. My dad followed us in his pickup because our couch, one of our few decent pieces of furniture, wouldn't squeeze into the Explorer.

They say the first year of marriage is the hardest, but that wasn't true for us. Our second year, the year we moved to Idaho, was *much* harder. It is one thing to get used to each other; it is another to get used to living with other people, especially when both of them are sick and struggling. We felt like we had become the parents of two 80-year-old children who were basically confined to their home.

Kim's grandparents had always been financially comfortable and very independent, and now they had a young couple living in their house. Grandpa had always been in charge, and now things were different. To have his granddaughter taking care of him was humiliating and made him uneasy at first. But it didn't take long for him to change his tune. We developed a rhythm. Kim did all the cooking, and I took care of the yard. Because her grandparents lived on three acres with a beautiful orchard, simple groundskeeping and yard maintenance were almost a full-time job. And I was good at it.

Sadly, Kim's grandfather didn't last long. He died only three months after our arrival, but I believe our help and presence made a difference in the last days of his life.

Meanwhile, I hadn't entirely given up on a career in the medical field, so I started to investigate the possibility of becoming an EMT, an emergency medical technician. In my mind it was the next best thing to being an emergency room physician, which had always been a strong interest of mine. I discovered that there was an EMT training course starting up locally, just down the street from our new home. Kim's parents thought it was a great idea for me to pursue this and gave us $700 so I could take the class.

Turns out, I was a natural. I caught onto everything quickly, and after six weeks I finished at the top of my class. Sixty-four people had started the program, and only 23 of us completed it. My instructor was so impressed with my grasp of what was required that he encouraged me to take the EMT-P course, which would start in another two weeks. This more advanced course would add the paramedic element, qualifying me for the highest level of emergency first responder work. Of course, it was much more extensive—and expensive—but once again Kim's parents loaned us the needed money to sign up for the year-and-a-half-long program.

I loved it from the very first class. My instructor was a witty, feisty, no-nonsense guy. He had 30 years as a paramedic under his belt, and he entertained us with story after story of his experiences. Every story contained bits of important information we needed. And he was hilarious, a born storyteller. He saw my passion and willingness to work hard, so he took me under his wing and gave me special attention. I had never enjoyed learning so much.

Still, it was hard work. Grueling, long hours of classroom instruction, reading, homework, and testing. I had to learn what it took to save someone's life. I had to be proficient at invasive interventions, endotracheal intubation, cricothyrotomy, IV administration, central lines, needle decompression, pharmacology, advanced anatomy, pathophysiology, toxicology, and recognizing cardiac dysrhythmias. In addition to classroom learning I was required to complete 200 hours of clinical experience, which involved vigorous rotations in the ER, labor and delivery, ICU, CCU, surgery, psychiatric ward, respiratory therapy, and general recovery. A paramedic needs to be ready for anything.

By the time I graduated I had performed 50 intubations and 100 IV insertions, and I had assisted at 50 live births and 15 C-sections. To top it all off, I completed 180 hours of practical rotations on the ambulance, where I operated as the paramedic in charge at the scene (under the guidance of a preceptor).

It was like cramming the whole experience of medical school into a year and a half, and I loved every moment of it.

While I was making my way through paramedic school, though, we faced some significant challenges.

Kim and I were still a newly wedded couple in a new city with no friends or social network, and we were wrapped up in taking care of Grandma—which, because of her condition, was not unlike taking care of a toddler. She needed constant attention.

And there was a lot of stress in our lives. Though I loved the paramedic program, it was very demanding. At the same time, I was trying to make a little money by helping Kim's dad, Greg, with his work as a landscape architect. Whenever he needed a little help he would call me, and I'd give him a hand with the installation of sprinkler systems, fountains, waterscapes, or whatever else he was working on. I was there mostly for the grunt work: digging holes and shoveling dirt. But I didn't mind. I've always enjoyed hard work. My years on the dairy farm had taught me about the feeling of accomplishment you get from really putting your back into manual labor.

Despite the stress and hard work, I had somehow managed to add 60 pounds to my weight in the first year of marriage. Evidently the physical exertion and ongoing stress weren't enough to balance out a diet that consisted primarily of sugar and carbs. When I got stressed, eating was one of my emotional crutches…and I was certainly under a good deal of stress.

One morning I tumbled out of bed and went to the bathroom, where I stepped on the scale to check my weight. I hadn't really been paying attention to how much weight I'd gained, so I was shocked when the numbers flashed back up at me: 300 pounds. Seeing those three digits was like having a siren go off in my head. I freaked out and instantly determined to make some changes.

After all, my mother had always struggled with obesity and health issues, and now it looked like I was preparing to follow in her footsteps. I was a health crisis waiting to happen, and it was time to do something about it.

I stomped downstairs to the kitchen, scavenged a big garbage bag from under the counter, and began purging the cupboards of all the unhealthy junk food that was lurking there. I was a man on a mission. If it was in a box or package, I tossed it, winging all the non-nutritious stuff into the bag. I was merciless, and it felt good to free myself of the stuff that was causing my weight to balloon at such an alarming rate.

Starting that very day, I changed my diet. I completely eradicated sugar and carbs, feasting instead on salad, vegetables, and lean meats. I joined the local gym and began going there nearly every day to use the elliptical and other fitness equipment. Without the help of a trainer I created my own intense fitness routine. This change in lifestyle, while not easy, had immediate benefits in how I felt, and the weight began to melt away. I would eventually lose 125 pounds.

Grandma's well-being and mental state continued to decline, and it put almost unmanageable pressure on Kim. She was quickly becoming an emotional basket case, and I knew something had to be done. With the blessing of her family, who understood the toll it was taking on us, we finally had to settle Kim's grandmother in a memory care facility. It was a hard decision to make, but we really had no other option.

By this point, we had developed a master plan for our future. I would finish my paramedic program, and then we could move back home to Oregon. So, after graduation I took my national registry and state tests, which I passed with flying colors. I was finally an officially licensed paramedic. It was time to put our plan into motion.

But then I discovered that a recent change in Oregon law had eliminated reciprocity. The change meant that Oregon no longer recognized a paramedic license from another state without a degree. I was furious and frustrated that all our plans would have to be reconsidered. If I wanted to be a paramedic, we were stuck in Idaho.

Initially I was really annoyed about how this affected our well-laid plans. But over the years I'd learned to accept that the Lord often works in mysterious ways. Within a few weeks I found a good job as a paramedic in Boise, Idaho, with a minimal starting wage. I was scheduled for two 24 hour shifts each week. I took to the work quickly and enjoyed getting to put what I had learned into practice. Kim found a job at a local credit union, and we were now officially a full-time working family. We were DINKs: "double income, no kids" people. Our only responsibility outside each other was our dog, Fletcher, a German short-haired pointer.

It didn't take long before we were doing well enough to purchase our first real home in Caldwell, Idaho, a nearby suburb. It was brand new and situated in a freshly minted subdivision—so new, in fact, that for a while we were the only house on our street. We started to make friends with other couples. It didn't take long before Idaho began to feel like home.

CHAPTER 12

NEVER DO ANYTHING YOU DON'T WANT TO HAVE TO EXPLAIN TO THE PARAMEDIC!

I could write a whole book just about my experiences as a paramedic. Every day I encountered something different; every day was a unique adventure. The best part of it all was that I felt like I was making a difference in people's lives. So many stories from that time in my life are permanently etched into my brain—catastrophic events, horrific sights, disturbing sounds, and stomach-turning smells. As a paramedic, I experienced life on an extreme plane, facing life-and-death situations day after day, so it played games with my subconscious and started to take a toll.

I won't soon forget how I felt on my first day as a newly minted paramedic with my state license, my bright blue medical kit, and my shiny EMT-P badge proudly displayed on my shirt. I was ready to roll. For the first three weeks I worked with an FTO, a field training officer named Greg who worked alongside me during my trial period, riding along to make sure I didn't make any costly mistakes. He was always available to intervene if necessary.

When the three weeks with the FTO ended, it meant I had completed the final phase of my on-the-job training. When I finished my last day with Greg, it was up to me to write up the report, which is required for each and every emergency call we answer. I was busy typing when Greg sauntered up behind me and loudly proclaimed, "Congratulations, you are *done*."

Since he was a jokester, I wasn't sure what he meant. Did I flunk out?

A smile came over Greg's face as he informed me that I had passed and he had officially "signed off" on me. He beamed like a proud older brother. So, starting at 7:30 a.m. the next morning I would be on my own, totally responsible for whatever situations arose and whatever decisions needed to be made in the spur of the moment.

On an ambulance shift there are usually two people. Of course, whoever gets chosen as your partner can make all the difference in what the job is like. It can be the best or worst part of the job. If you don't get along well, the shift can crawl by like molasses. If your partner becomes a friend, then the time flies by much more quickly.

Sometimes my partner was a fellow paramedic, but other times they were solely an EMT. I liked it best when I was partnered with a fellow paramedic because we could share some of the decision-making responsibilities in challenging medical situations. Two heads are always better than one. But if my partner was solely an EMT, then it was all on me. Paramedic or EMT, though, I needed someone who had my back and was a dependable person. Working well together always made situations go much more smoothly.

The daily routine of a paramedic is totally unpredictable. It can best be summed up as "hours of boredom interrupted by moments of sheer terror," as the saying goes. This is not an exaggeration. My first days on the job had plenty of excitement and more than a little terror, and I found myself a witness to people enduring the most extreme situations. These circumstances tended to bring out the best and worst in people.

As a paramedic, I learned a lot about human beings. How different we all are, and how differently we respond to situations. Given the same set of circumstances, people will respond in their different ways. I was witness to strength and calm, weakness and panic. I saw fear in its most extreme forms. Every call I responded to was unique, and I had to be quick to adapt to a new scenario in the blink of an eye.

The best calls were those that were relatively benign, where I could make a difference quickly because it really wasn't much of an emergency. Sometimes I even found myself in situations where it was hard to hold back my laughter on discovering the ridiculous situations people had gotten themselves into.

I won't soon forget my first day as a fully authorized paramedic.

I arrived a little early at the station (we all tried to do this as a courtesy to the crew who had worked through the night before, since our shifts started at 7:30 a.m. and ran until the same time the next morning). As I checked in I discovered that my partner for the shift was already there. It was Robert, who was a great guy, but he only had EMT training, which meant that I would be thrown into the deep end. On my first day I would be responsible for any advanced medical issues that needed attention, and I wouldn't have much backup. This made me a little nervous, but I was also excited about being able to prove myself right away.

Robert and I started to do a check of the ambulance to make sure we had plenty of all the usual medical supplies, when suddenly we heard the unmistakable beeping tones that let us know that something was up: "Beep, beep, beep, beep, beep...Engine 10, Medic 60... Assist PD with an auto accident...Highway 44 and Old State Street."

I breathed a sigh of relief. This dispatcher's call to "assist PD with an auto accident" would typically indicate that we were dealing with a fender bender, and we were just being asked to join the police officer at the scene. Such a call would usually end up being one where we didn't deal with a patient. Many times, in fact, the call would end up being canceled before we even got there.

Robert and I strapped ourselves in and hit "F9" on the mobile data terminal to confirm that we were en route. In my mind I pondered the location of the accident. It was at an intersection where people were normally traveling fast. The speed limit there was 60 miles per hour. If no one was injured, it would be kind of miraculous.

As we drove down the street and out of sight of the station, the dispatcher returned with an update: "Dispatch, Medic 60, upgrade to code 3... You have two patients...one red, and one potential fatality."

My stomach knotted up. A "red" patient means someone who is critically injured, facing the serious possibility of death. I picked up the mic and called for backup. Before I even put the mic back down I heard the words, "Medic 1 already en route." I called for another ambulance in case we needed additional support.

And then I said a quick prayer. For clarity of mind and for God's help with what lay ahead. I literally remember praying, "Oh Jesus, please help me not to choke."

As we pulled up to the scene, my first thought was that it would be a miracle if anyone had survived. There was a small four-door sedan wrapped around a large, steel telephone pole. Since it had struck the pole head-on at a high speed, it was now almost unrecognizable as a car. It looked like a twisted pretzel of metal and plastic, and there was glass everywhere. Pieces of debris were scattered across the highway, and black smoke rose from the wreckage. The vehicle had collided with the telephone pole with such force that the front grille was now all the way in the backseat.

The passengers of the vehicle were one adult male and one adult female. I later learned that they had been out partying through the previous night and were both severely intoxicated. The driver had lost control while trying to negotiate a turn at high speed.

An off-duty paramedic had witnessed the entire incident and had been able to respond immediately. When we arrived he was already taking care of the male patient on the driver's side, so I went to the passenger's side and peered in. I couldn't see much, as the interior was collapsed and mangled and filled with smoke and dust. I caught a glimpse of some blonde hair. There was no way to open the door and rescue her, so the fire department, which had just arrived, started to cut the car apart to get her out.

I reached in through the window to see if I could get a pulse. Though I still couldn't see her whole body, I saw enough to be able to put my fingers on her neck. Yes, there was a very faint pulse. I told Robert to prepare the EKG monitor and the intubation kit. It took about 25 crucial minutes using the jaws of life, to release her from the vehicle after which we carefully laid her out on the pavement. Her face was covered by her long blonde hair. I knelt beside her and moved it aside to secure an airway. As I brushed aside her hair, I gasped at what I saw.

The kinetic energy created by the impact had literally shattered her head, cracking her face wide open from the top of her skull down to her lower jaw. The brutal image reminded me of what happens when you bust open a pumpkin or a watermelon. A shattered exterior, exposing brains, eyeballs, bone fragments and teeth. Mercifully, she had certainly become unconscious on impact. I froze for a moment, my face draining of color and a feeling of horror and shock overcoming my senses. I didn't know how to handle what I was seeing. Trying to calm myself I looked again inside the now opened vehicle. There were her shoes, perfectly in place and looking like she had just slipped them off. And there was her cell phone lying on the floorboard.

Suddenly the cell phone came to life. The victim was receiving a call. I saw the caller ID clearly: "MOM." The enormity of it all was overwhelming.

Then, like a guardian angel, I felt the comforting hand of one of my more experienced colleagues on my shoulder. He could see that I was losing my composure and was visibly trembling. He helped me up and said, "Go. Go sit in the ambulance."

I did what he said. I walked straight over to the ambulance and climbed in, closing the door behind me so I could take a moment to compose myself.

Instead, I began to sob. I couldn't even begin to contain the waves of emotion that swept over me. I dropped my head down between my knees as I wrestled with the heaving tears and the nausea that was taking hold. Thoughts of regret and despair ravaged my mind as I began to ask myself, *What the heck just happened?* I had just glimpsed death in all its ugliness, and I hadn't been able to deal with it. This was my first-ever call, and I cringed at the thought of ever going on another one.

I later learned that such an experience is a common rite of passage along the path to becoming a confident paramedic. Most people have to face down a totally disturbing sight or two before they can begin to handle it well, before their mind and heart can deal with it and move on. I just happened to get my baptism of fire on my very first day.

If this is what it would be like as a paramedic, I wondered if I had made the biggest mistake of my life.

I'd like to tell you that things settled down after that first horrible call, but they did not! I received a trial-by-fire introduction to the world of the paramedic, and the sternest on-the-job wake-up call one could imagine. Though life didn't settle down, I slowly became accustomed to the work. In fact, it seemed like I was destined to get most of the crazy and ugly calls over the next months and years. My coworkers even noticed that I was the one regularly getting called to the worst imaginable situations, and I believe some of them probably breathed a sigh of relief when they found they weren't working with me on a shift. I remember some of my partners making a "cross" in the air with their fingers when they saw my name on the schedule, hoping not to get teamed up with me. It was almost like I was bad luck or something, and at times it felt like that black cloud of death followed me, buzzing around like flies on a piece of dog doo-doo. I quickly earned the nickname "the crap magnet."

I went on one horrific call after another. Wrecks with mangled bodies and missing limbs and even decapitations. Drownings. Suicides by hanging or self-inflicted gunshot wounds. Countless drug overdoses. Burn victims. Stroke victims. You name it, and I saw it. The very worst calls were those involving babies or small children who had been killed or victimized by abuse. Sometimes I was even in danger myself when dealing with psychotic patients or drug-crazed tweakers and hoodlums who would get violent and turn on me and my partner, attempting to fight or even kill us. There were moments where it felt as though it was me or them—life or death.

Can you ever get used to seeing and experiencing such stuff? Probably not. I never totally became numb to it, but over time it started to bother me less and less. Eventually I got kind of calloused to the kind of emotional trauma I experienced on that first call. By year five I was no longer rattled by what had affected me so much during year one.

And despite all the emotional challenges, I really did love my job. Once I acclimated to working in the pressure cooker of life-and-death situations day after day I found it very fulfilling. I was proud that I had accomplished the goal I had set for myself, and I quickly became very competent at dealing with all the unpredictable scenarios that came my way every single day. I learned to feed off the stress and transform it into passion for the work I was doing.

Sometimes, like on my first call, the patient would already be dead when I arrived. The scary situations, though, involved those who were barely holding on. Sometimes I could help them pull through. Sometimes they didn't make it despite my best efforts. Perhaps scariest of all were the victims with chronic asthma, emphysema, or COPD (Chronic Obstructive Pulmonary Disease). When people can't breathe they panic or become extremely volatile. Such a patient can be difficult to manage. When a patient's airway fails, they often cease breathing and go into full-blown cardiac arrest. I would have to try to keep them calm and get them breathing normally again, which is often a tall order—and sometimes just impossible.

Over time I became a very good paramedic. I'd worked with all kinds of situations without a single accusation of medical malpractice and had never been written up or reprimanded. In fact, I had a slew of "medical excellence" forms in my file which had been written by our physician medical directors, and I'd even received a certified letter of excellence from the hospital board at Saint Luke's Regional Medical Center because I had set a record for having the quickest "field to cath lab" response in their history. I was fast, I was effective, and I had an eye for recognizing critical problems.

The other great thing about my job was the people with whom I got to work. My partners soon became like a family to me. Most of them were amazing people—people who were unreservedly committed to helping others.

It is that commitment that keeps a paramedic going, not the money!

One evening I was partnered with Mark, and we got dispatched to another "assist PD" call. This time it was a "welfare check," which is when a concerned neighbor calls because they haven't seen their friend in a while and the family hasn't been able to contact them either. When this happens, the police are called in, and they like to have the paramedics meet them at the house just in case. Often someone who has been missing in action has a serious medical need.

We showed up at a dingy old trailer park, tucked away behind a nicer housing development. The police officer was already on the scene and informed us that the occupant of the trailer hadn't been seen coming or going for about five days. The family lived out of town and were concerned that they hadn't been able to reach the woman who lived here.

We checked the door and found it locked. There was a stack of mail piling up outside, which indicated that the lady hadn't been out through the main entrance for several days. While Mark tried shouting through the front door, I went around to the side of the trailer and peered in through the window. It was dark inside, but I could see a woman sitting in a recliner, watching television. I assumed she was just chilling out in front of the tube. I banged on the window, but I couldn't seem to get her attention.

The fire department helped us pop open the door with a metal bar, but it caught when it hit the end of the security chain. Even having it open just a couple inches, though, told us what we needed to know. An overpowering stench greeted us, as well as the sound of escaping flies.

Mark discovered a side window in the kitchen that wasn't locked and crawled in through it. From outside I could hear the unmistakable sounds of gagging and a small dog barking frantically. When Mark undid the latch and let us in the front door he had his jacket over half his face, trying to stifle the overwhelming smell of death. He gasped for some fresh air and then re-entered with me.

The house was completely dark except for the television set, which was playing a rerun of *I Love Lucy*. But the scene before us was more like something from the movie *Seven*—you know, the "sloth" victim who was chained to the bed. The victim was sitting in her recliner facing the television. Drawing closer, I saw that she appeared to be emaciated, and her face looked disfigured. When I shined my flashlight on it I saw that one side had been partially eaten away, evidently by her little Jack Russell terrier who had become so hungry that, out of desperation, he had chewed into her face. Clearly, she was dead.

As the others shuffled out through the front door, I picked up my radio to call the coroner. Then I realized that none of us had officially physically assessed the patient or checked for a pulse. I put the radio back on my belt and crept back over to her chair, my nose and mouth covered by my jacket. I reached down to touch her neck so I could officially report that "the patient had no pulse." A shiver went down my spine. It felt like that scene in *Indiana Jones and the Temple of Doom*, where Kate Capshaw's character has to put her hand in that gooey, bug-infested hole.

When I gingerly touched the woman's neck, she startled into consciousness. She wasn't dead! She gasped for air, then began writhing and moaning.

She wasn't the only one startled. I nearly jumped out of my skin. I yelled to Mark, "She's still alive!"

With his help, I loaded the woman onto the stretcher and into the ambulance for the ride to the hospital. Since she needed a lot of immediate attention, we got one of the firemen on the scene to drive the vehicle. In the back of the ambulance I intubated her and began ventilations, and Mark got an IV started. The woman was still alive when we arrived at the hospital, but sadly, she died two days later.

We learned from the attending physician that she had suffered a massive stroke several days earlier and had been totally paralyzed due to a herniating blood vessel inside her head. Because she was unable to move she couldn't call for help. It was unthinkably awful. And for some time afterward, the joke around the station was that I was the one who had gone out on the *Dawn of the Dead* call.

Not surprisingly, the national statistical burnout rate for a paramedic is between one and three years. The ones who make it longer than that are an anomaly. The level of physical and emotional stress of the job is not something that most human beings are able to maintain long term. To survive, you must become guarded, which is a nice way to say, you become hard.

I made it beyond the average, but by my sixth year I could feel how much I had built a wall around my heart to cope with all the horrors I'd experienced. One day, as I was sitting down in the shower trying to rinse off the smell of burned human flesh, Kim said to me, "What's wrong with you? You're not even the same person anymore."

I knew she was right, but this was my job, and I intended to stick it out until I got my pension. Hey, what was another 20 years of living in a horror film? I'd passed my fifth year, which meant that I was fully vested and had full access to my 401(k). I'd been putting money back each month, which was good, since I was tired and severely in danger of total burnout.

In that sixth year I began to wonder how long I could keep going. At the same time, the old dreams of making music had slowly begun to resurface. I had buried them deep, but like the poor woman we found in front of the TV, they refused to die.

I asked the Lord to give me back the tender heart that I had largely lost. I asked Him to revive the dreams of making music for Him. And I held on to this promise: "Delight yourself in the LORD; and He will give you the desires of your heart" (Psalm 37:4). I made this prayer my personal mantra, but I had no idea the lengths God would go to in answering it.

CHAPTER 13

THE LIGHTNING AND THE THUNDER

Something was in the air...

Maybe it was time for a change. My dream of a full-time music career had re-emerged with a vengeance, and I was praying that God would open some sort of door. Actually, I was pretty much begging Him for that to happen. I knew there were probably a lot of people who had the same dream, but that didn't stop me.

I started to use my days off to dust off my guitar skills, and I began to write songs again. I was really enjoying being back in the musical groove, and I even played an occasional acoustic night at the local coffee shops in Boise. When I really began concentrating on songwriting again, I felt things click. I realized that I could communicate what I wanted to say through my songs even better than before.

God had taught me so much through my experiences of the previous few years: about the human condition, about pain and suffering, about God's grace and presence with us in the darkest moments of our lives, and about the only real source of hope during such times.

Something was in the air on that relatively calm October day...

That something was an oncoming storm.

Which brings me back to where this book started.

Following our call about the lightning strike I found myself in the back of the ambulance, fighting to try to save the life of the young woman who had been struck by lightning. And I wasn't hopeful about the outcome, though I prayed as I tried to do anything I could think of to revive her. Just 20 minutes prior it had been another routine day at work, but now here I was in the back of the ambulance with a young woman—a victim of a lightning strike—whose life seemed to have slipped away. I didn't know how I could help her. At this point, I didn't really think she could be saved.

Randall and I had been in the closest unit, but it still took us ten minutes (driving fast) to get to the scene of the incident. Ten minutes is a long time when it comes to emergency response, as there is only a small window of time when CPR can be effective. If CPR isn't performed almost immediately, the likelihood of resuscitation decreases drastically. I knew even before we arrived on the scene that it would likely be too late. And so it appeared.

I later learned that the victim was Lara Eustermann, a healthy and athletic woman and the owner of a successful catering and event-planning business. She and her husband were doing well enough financially that they were looking for a piece of property in the hills surrounding Boise where they could build their dream home.

The day of the accident Lara had loaded her mother and two little boys into their SUV to go look at some land in the Hidden Springs area. The rain had kicked up suddenly while they were walking around and exploring the property. As the downpour turned into a torrent, they all started running for the shelter of the SUV.

Suddenly there was a bright flash all around them and an explosion that knocked them off their feet. Dazed and confused, Lara's mother got to her feet and noticed that Lara was lying in the grass. As she moved closer, she gasped aloud. Lara had been struck by a bolt of lightning. There was a large entrance wound on the top of her head. The electricity had entered the top of her head and traveled through her body, exiting through her right ankle.

Lara's mother dialed 911 on her cell phone and administered CPR, kneeling beside the unmoving body of her daughter. She quickly realized this wasn't accomplishing anything and her mind raced through her options. None of them seemed good. She just hoped the ambulance would arrive quickly.

This was the series of events that preceded our arrival at the scene.

There in the back of ambulance, as we sped toward the hospital, I believed that Lara would likely be pronounced dead by the time we arrived. I breathed a wordless prayer for her to pull through and sought to stabilize her somehow. I inserted a breathing tube into her lungs and started ventilating her with a bag-valve mask. She also had an IV in each arm and EKG pads on her chest. The initial EKG showed a fatal rhythm—her heart was just weakly quivering, not sending blood through her body as it should. If this cardiac rhythm didn't change soon, she would be dead. Randall administered manual chest compressions to nudge her heart toward beating fully on its own.

About five minutes into the drive I noticed that the EKG was starting to register a normal heart rhythm, meaning that blood was flowing again.

I was flabbergasted. I had never seen anyone return from a state like the one in which Lara had been. I shook my head in disbelief and double-checked the connections on the equipment. Unreal. I got a blank, surprised stare on my face, just like Wile E. Coyote has in that moment, suspended in midair, before he plunges off the cliff and rushes toward the ground below. But unlike Wile E. Coyote's shock, this was the best kind of surprise.

I began to check Lara's other vital signs. The oxygen monitor was reading an almost perfect 99 percent. Her blood pressure was an amazing 120/70. She was literally returning from the dead.

By the time we arrived at the hospital, it looked like she might pull through.

Lara was in the ICU, on a ventilator for three days and in a coma for almost three weeks. Then she spent more than two months in rehabilitation at Elks Rehab. Because of the intense electrical charge that had roared through her body, as well as her initial oxygen deprivation, she'd suffered some severe neuralgic damage and was unable to walk for a month. It was a long road back to normal, but her survival was nothing less than a miracle

Soon the story of Lara's incredible survival and recovery was not only shared on the local television network, but on media outlets throughout the country. Everyone wanted to interview this survivor of a lightning strike. She was interviewed a couple of times by Matt Lauer on the *Today* show and also was a guest with Larry King on his program. One day I caught the end of an interview with Lara as I switched on the television set. Now that the realities of her new life had settled in, she was obviously very upset. She had tears in her eyes as she talked about how much her life had changed and the realization that it would never be the same again. She was now semiparalyzed and felt trapped in a crippled body. Her mental faculties had not been affected, and she was grateful to be alive, but she was grieving over how much she had lost and experiencing a lot of fear about what lay ahead.

As I watched, I wondered if I had done her a favor by resuscitating her.

Several months later there was a midmorning awards ceremony for Ada County paramedics to showcase some of the noteworthy rescues

that had made a difference in the lives of people from the community. Some of the patients were also invited so they could be publicly honored for their strength and courage in coming through such traumatic events.

Since Lara's story had received so much attention, both she and I were being honored that day. It gave me the first real chance to meet her face-to-face since our momentous ambulance ride together. Other than me popping into her hospital room to leave some flowers when she was in rehabilitation, we hadn't seen each other. But she had continued to make a surprising recovery—beyond what anyone would have expected.

Our conversation at that event led to more conversations, a few meetings over coffee, and even dinners together with our spouses. A real friendship developed.

I don't know if it's common for a rescuer and the person who is rescued to forge some sort of bond in the experience of facing down potential death together, but this happened for Lara and me. We got a chance to know each other as people and learn about the stories that had brought each of us to that fateful day.

As a Christian, I don't believe in coincidences. I was a devout follower of Jesus, and Lara was not—but that didn't matter. I believed then, and still do, that God put her into my life for a reason, and that I was in her life for a reason too. I would soon realize one of the purposes why God had woven her story into mine.

During our conversations, one of the things I learned about Lara is that she is a curious person. Someone who asks lots of questions. She was really interested in learning more about who I was and what I wanted to do with my life.

One day we were talking over coffee, and she was sharing very vulnerably about how much sadness she felt about no longer being able to operate her catering business. She felt crushed by the loss of something she enjoyed and that had brought her such fulfillment. I could tell that the feelings went deep and that even talking about the situation was very emotional for her. And when she clearly didn't want to talk about her own issues anymore, she wiped the tears from her eyes with the back of her hand and reached over to pluck a tissue from its box. She locked eyes with me and asked, "Ryan, if you weren't a paramedic, what would you be doing instead? What's your dream?"

There was a pause, then she continued, "What would you do if you could do *anything*? I just see something more in you; something behind the scenes that always seems to be tugging at you. I see it."

Here was a woman who didn't know me that well and who didn't share my faith. But it seemed like God was speaking to me through her—prophesying right into my life.

The answer came spilling out of me without a moment of hesitation. "Music. I want to play music full time for a living, and I want to help people with my songs."

She settled back in her chair and pondered my answer for a moment. "Music? Okay, how would one go about doing that? What would it look like to make a living from singing? What steps would it take to get there?" She was cutting right to the core of my answer.

I shared with her how I visualized it could happen. The first step would be to record my songs. I'd written a lot of them over the past ten years, and many of them seemed like good ones. I had the material I needed just waiting to be recorded. When I thought about it, there were five songs in which I had the fullest confidence. I knew they were strong. What I needed to do was get them recorded on a professional demo, which I could then send out to record companies.

Lara and I chatted some more about how music moves people's hearts, about the music business, and about how much work it takes to be a success. We finished our coffee, and as we pushed back our chairs, she leaned on her cane and hobbled over to me. She gave me a big, encouraging hug. I saw again the incredible strength of this woman who was fighting to figure out how to live a normal life, and here she was—concerned about me and my dreams.

As we walked through the front door, she stopped so she could say one more thing. I could tell that it was important to her for me to realize how serious she was about her next words. "If I can ever help you, in any way, just say the word and I'll be there. I wanna be there for you."

I smiled a sheepish smile. "Okay," I responded. But I doubted that I would ever take her up on the offer. I had just been doing my job when I helped save her life. Besides, I don't really like to impose on anybody for anything. I can take care of myself. She had no obligation to me. Still, the words were so kind and sincere that they raised my spirits as I climbed back in my car to drive home.

CHAPTER 14

BREAKTHROUGH

I'd found myself thinking about music more than ever, and I finally decided it was time to do something about my dreams. I put together a band, and every weekend that I didn't have paramedic duty we'd be out playing music all around the area, taking advantage of any opportunity to share our songs. We'd load our equipment into my minivan and go wherever we could arrange a gig.

At first, my bandmates—Jeremy, Mandy, and Pru—and I were doing local concerts, but before long we started playing music all over the Pacific Northwest, mostly at small churches. It felt so good to be back at it, and our band of quirky renegades bonded together as a tight music-making entity and as friends. Actually, we were more than friends. We became like a family.

A local buzz about our music began to build, and people started getting excited about what we were doing. Not long after my memorable conversation with Lara, I got a call from a local concert promoter who wanted me to be a part of a "Christian battle of the bands" he was organizing for the Idaho State Fair. My initial response was pretty dismissive. It just didn't sound like something I wanted to do. But the promoter was desperate. He explained that he needed ten bands to get approval for the event from the fair board. He had lined up nine bands and needed one more or the board was going to cancel the event. He was pressing me, virtually begging.

I'm glad he couldn't see my face on the other end of the line. I rolled my eyes, and I'm sure my expression was a mix of annoyance and disdain. *After all,* I thought to myself, *I'm trying to be a professional musician. I don't want to go play with a bunch of punk kids at the fair, on a hot afternoon, at the gazebo right next to the horse barn.* That sounded kind of humiliating. Wasn't it beneath me to be slugging it out musically against a bunch of amateurs at the state fair?

Then I felt that still, small, peaceful voice whispering in my ear, just like it had at so many other junctures in my life: "You need to do this." Immediately I realized that I was being proud and self-centered, and I couldn't ignore the heavenly nudge.

I let out an audible sigh of resignation and told the promoter that we would participate. He was ecstatic.

That meant we'd be plugging in our equipment on a stage where the smell of horse manure would waft over the audience. Prestigious opportunity? No. An act of obedience? Yes.

When the day of our performance came, it was every bit as hot as I'd dreaded. The smell was just as pungent as I'd imagined. As we unloaded our gear, two things were clear. One, this stage was located a long way from where all the action was; we were in a gazebo in the middle of nowhere on the fairgrounds. Two, there was hardly anyone to witness the show. Other than the other bands, there was hardly a single fan in the audience. It was mostly just a few proud, wide-eyed parents who had come to cheer on their kids as they played.

Well, I thought, *let's just get this over with.* At least I didn't have to worry about anyone important being in the crowd to witness us making fools out of ourselves in view (and in olfactory range) of the horse stables. By the time we were scheduled to play our set—the last to take the stage—the crowd had swollen to maybe 30 people. But we played well and just focused on doing what we knew how to do: make good music.

After our set, the three judges huddled together and then announced the winners. My band and I watched as third and second places were awarded to other bands. Then, rather solemnly and with a tone of drama and inappropriate importance: "First place goes to the Ryan Stevenson Band!"

There was a silver lining to the whole experience: The prize for first place was $1,000 and some time at a local recording studio. I recognized the name of the place. It was a reputable one; a place I'd wanted to record at for a long time. I'd never had the extra money, though, to make it a reality.

My pride and arrogance had nearly cost me a great opportunity. I was glad I had listened to that gentle voice, even when my attitude wasn't that good.

By my calculations, if we wanted to do this right, the award money would only be enough for us to record a single song. I had hoped to create an EP with five songs. I chatted with one of the judges, who was also the owner of this studio. He told me that it would take $5,000 to record five songs if we wanted to do it right. And I did—but I had no idea how I could come up with another $4,000. I certainly didn't have that kind of money lying around, and my band was doing little more than breaking even on our shows.

So how was I going to get the rest of the money I needed? My foot was in the door, but I needed cash to push it open the rest of the way. I was so desperate that I even considered asking my father-in-law for another loan. Or maybe offering to work it off in his landscape business. I was more than willing to dig holes and move dirt to make this opportunity a reality. But he had already done so much to help with the costs of paramedic school that I couldn't bring myself to ask.

I was driving home from worship team practice when a crazy little thought popped into my mind. Hadn't Lara said, not more than a few weeks before, "If I can ever help you, in any way, just say the word and I'll be there"?

No, I thought to myself immediately, *I could never ask her*. But the idea remained, and I kept replaying our conversation. *Is it possible? No. Should I? No. Might she? Well, maybe she would.*

I pulled into my driveway, and instead of going inside I just sat there. Then I got out of the car and went to the front steps, holding my cell phone in my hands. I started sweating. I moved the phone from one hand to the other. I argued with myself. I couldn't even believe I was considering this option. I told myself, "There's no way I am going to call her about this," even as my fingers, seemingly on autopilot, were dialing the number and putting the phone to my ear.

Lara picked up on the first ring. After all, it was her favorite paramedic calling. I couldn't get out much more than, "Hello..."

She seemed glad to hear my voice, and this gave me the courage I needed to spit out my request. I imagine she heard a pretty rapid string of words as I told her that I'd won a battle of the bands competition and had been awarded some money and studio time to record my songs, but that it wasn't enough to cover the full cost. I was elated at the opportunity but didn't know how I could get the rest of the money together.

I could sense her smile from the tone in her voice as she told me about an interesting turn of events in her life. Just a few weeks earlier she had received a completely unexpected check in the mail—some sort of retroactive disability payment she hadn't known was coming. She still hadn't had a chance to go out and cash the check or put it in the bank. It was sitting on her computer keyboard, out of sight and out of mind.

Lara had no idea what it might cost to make a record. She figured it was probably tens of thousands of dollars. She was surprised when I told her that I needed $4,000. There was silence on the other end of line, followed by a little squeal. The uncashed check, she informed me, was for that exact amount: $4,000.00! She hadn't thought about what she was going to do with the money, and she didn't need it for anything in particular. "Now," she said, "I know exactly what it is for. This is your check." She wouldn't take no for an answer. She demanded that I accept the money and use it to chase my musical dream.

It was a miracle, and it came through someone who didn't even necessarily believe in miracles.

I was undone, and I was grateful. Over the next few weeks I coproduced and recorded five of my songs in the studio in Boise. Once we had laid down the tracks and got them sounding the way I wanted, I sent the demo to my friend Chris Stevens, who was living in Nashville and working with TobyMac—the same singer whose performance at Jesus Northwest had given birth to my dreams. Chris did an amazing job at adding the gloss the recording needed.

Next, I forwarded the demo to a friend who worked at BEC Recordings in Seattle. A day or two later I learned that they wanted to sign me to their record company and release one of the songs—"Yesterday, Today, Forever"—as a single for Christian radio.

Lara was so different from me in so many ways. I was a person of faith and she still had lots of questions about God. Our politics mostly lined up on opposite sides of the aisle. We just didn't have that much in common. But she showed me a kind of love and grace and kindness that I hadn't often experienced in my life. Her gift changed the course of my life. I'd been her "angel" in the back of that ambulance, but now she was my "angel," sent by God to bless me and put me on the road to singing full time. There would still be some bumps in that road, but now I was finally on the path to pursuing my calling.

God loves to surprise us. His gifts often come from the most unexpected sources and in the most unanticipated ways. If we can just be patient and keep trusting, He will not fail us. This kind-hearted woman, whom I had met in the worst imaginable circumstances, had shifted the trajectory of my life through her generosity. In the back of the ambulance, working to try to save her life, I never would have known that I was also saving my own. She was a gift wrapped in thunder and lightning.

CHAPTER 15

CROSSROADS

The easiest thing for any human to do is doubt. We are all driven by our emotions, and our emotions are always experiencing a series of ups and downs. We find ourselves on peaks and in valleys, caught between hope and despair, joy and depression. And our circumstances are also continually in flux. One day things are going great, and the next we find ourselves struggling.

Life is a roller coaster.

Since we are always tempted to base our emotional responses only on what we can see at a moment in time, we struggle with doubts. This isn't helped much by the emotional baggage we carry from our past, which threatens the present because of our brokenness. We must somehow learn how to deal with that baggage. We can't just ignore it or wish it away, because it will always have a subtle influence on our marriage, our career, our calling, our personality, and even our relationship with God. Unless our brokenness gets healed, it will affect how we think and feel and act every day.

We want to see that healing, that brokenness, get taken care of in a miraculous moment where God intervenes and changes everything immediately. But that just isn't the way He usually works.

The Christian life is all about faith. The book of Hebrews defines faith succinctly and unforgettably: "Now faith is the assurance of things hoped for, the conviction of things not seen" (11:1). I love this verse, as it is a powerful reminder that God is at work even in those times where we don't see it or can't feel it. Everything ultimately comes down to trust.

This is such a great comfort when I'm in a season where it feels hard to hold on. It means that when God calls me to do something, I don't have to wait for all the "signs" to align. I must step out in obedience and act on His calling. This is important. As James 2:17 reminds us, faith without action is dead. Our faith must keep moving forward, even when we don't see the future clearly or feel a spark of internal confirmation that we are doing the right thing. Often, we need to follow for the kingdom's sake even when the final result isn't in view.

The promise that strengthens me as I walk the path of faith is the one found in Jeremiah 29:11: " 'I know the plans I have for you,' declares the Lord, 'plans to prosper you and not to harm you, plans to give you hope and a future' " (NIV). Our hope for the future isn't based on the wisdom and efficacy of our own plans, but upon God's. He knows us better than we know ourselves—and He understands our thoughts, feelings, and fears. He works in all the circumstances of our lives in order to stretch us, bend us, purify us, and refine us. He has plans for us. Sometimes, however, those plans will take us through the fire.

If you want to produce a fine wine, you must crush and press and filter the grapes before you can extract what is inside them. God takes us through a process not unlike what the grapes go through. His goal is to transform us from dusty old grapes hanging around on a vine into an invigorating and intoxicating witness for Him.

God was continuing to work with me. My relationship with Kim was relatively healthy, but sometimes my insecurities and guilt would flare up once again and create problems for us. I had not really dealt with the regrets and shame of my past, and I often was tormented by a nagging voice of guilt. I didn't want to burden Kim with my issues, so I wouldn't really talk much about what was going on inside me. The result was that I kept cycling through periods of massive insecurity and self-doubt and shame, and this always had a detrimental effect on us as a couple. It was exhausting and confusing.

The way Kim continued to respond to me is evidence of what an amazing person she is. She knew when she married me that I was pretty messed up in a lot of ways. She understood what she had signed up for when she had said yes to our marriage. But even with all her patience, I think she finally began to get tired of dealing with all my unhealthy cycles of emotional struggle. Still, she never demanded that I go see a counselor or tried to manipulate or pressure me in any way. On the other hand, she had no hesitation about calling me out when I needed a strong dose of the truth.

Even as my musical aspirations took shape, I was still a mess inside. I was totally excited about the doors that were opening, but I was also a scared and insecure little child inside who didn't believe I deserved this success and who couldn't fully feel confident in my gifts. Holding the contract for a record deal in my hand, I was happy. At the same time, I was assaulted by the persistent inner voices of doubt. *If people knew who you really were inside, they wouldn't love or respect you*, they whispered. And, *You're a phony. You're not authentic. Who are you to represent God?* I couldn't just ignore the voices, for I was convinced that there was a lot of truth in these words.

When it looked like things were starting to come together in my life and career, I was so overcome by self-doubt that I felt almost suicidal. It was hard to move forward when I was dragging so much emotional baggage along behind me. The voices were getting to be more than I could handle. So I finally did what I had needed to do for so very long.

One day, driving home, the emotions started churning to the point where I thought I was going to snap. Then the inner voices started in again. I couldn't handle it anymore. I was just exhausted.

I recognized I was at some sort of crossroads. I knew beyond a shadow of a doubt that I needed to be healed in my heart and soul. I pulled into the driveway at home, switched off the engine, put my head down against the steering wheel, and started weeping. Between my sobs I managed to put together a prayer: "Jesus, please fix me. I need you to break through the madness inside me. I need You to expose the lies and help me understand the truth about how You think about me. I need to know that You are my Dad and I'm Your son. I don't care what it looks like, and I don't care what it feels like. Jesus, please, do whatever You need to do to heal me."

My prayer wasn't eloquent, but it expressed the deepest desire of my heart: to be changed. I knew that I couldn't fix myself. I had tried for years. I'd attempted to ignore what I was feeling and push it all down inside. I'd mustered all the strength within me to resist the voice of the Enemy. I'd hoped things would just get better on their own. But now I was doing what I should have done so long ago—lay all my brokenness at His feet and trust Him to fix me.

I can't tell you I was completely changed in an instant, but God really did something in my heart at that very moment. He reached down deep into my brokenness and began the process of piecing me back together. I had opened up to Him with a completely honest invitation for Him to do "whatever it takes," and He had accepted that invitation.

But honestly, I don't think I was fully prepared for what that might mean.

CHAPTER 16

HEAVEN BOUND

One of the most challenging things about our move to Idaho had been leaving my mother behind. She had been diagnosed with cancer when I was a sophomore in high school, and since then she had undergone a series of surgeries, treatments, radiation, and chemotherapy, which had led to a temporary remission.

A few years after these treatments, Mom was in a small car accident. It was a fender bender, but the force of the impact had thrust her violently forward into the steering wheel, injuring her sternum. For weeks after the accident she continued to have an intense pain in her chest, which increased in severity whenever she moved her arms or coughed. When the pain got to be too much and seemed like it wasn't getting any better, she went back to the doctor. She knew something was wrong.

Indeed, it was. The cancer had flared up again, and this time it had spread into her bones and throughout her body. The prognosis was grim: incurable and inoperable bone cancer.

Her oncologist advised her to try a new treatment option that he claimed wouldn't rid her of the cancer but would at least slow its growth and prolong her life. Being the optimist that she was, Mom jumped at this chance and began bimonthly treatments with a brand-new drug called Zometa. This drug was not designed to kill the cancer, but to coat and strengthen the bones so the cancer can't eat away at them so rapidly. It was a matter of buying some extra time, and that was certainly worth a try.

Still, the clock was ticking.

Mom kept up a positive attitude as she checked herself in every two weeks for an infusion of Zometa. They'd settle her in a comfortable recliner for an hour as they pumped it into her system. During that hour she would chat happily with the doctors and other cancer patients. Everyone found her attitude to be uplifting and encouraging. She had a gift for kindness and caring for others, and in this situation that gift manifested itself in abundance. She was clearly more concerned with what others were going through than with her own pain.

After each treatment, though, she would be sick for days. The Zometa was hard on her system. She'd become violently ill and confined to her bed for about a week, then she'd perk up and start feeling more like herself again. Soon, she'd have to return for another treatment and go through it all over again. It was an exhausting and debilitating cycle, but she was committed to living for as long as she could. She wanted to be around her family.

For the most part, I had to watch this process from a distance. It was a seven-hour uninterrupted drive to get from Boise to Bonanza, so I couldn't take it very often. Getting time off work was a challenge. But every time I was able to return to Bonanza I found Mom looking a little worse. The cancer was slowly taking its toll. Her eyes had lost much of their usual sparkle, and she looked increasingly weary. I knew the day was approaching all too rapidly when I would lose her for good.

Even if I couldn't visit as often as I wanted, there was always the phone. Mom would often call me up in the morning for a brief chat.

One morning, after making the usual small talk, she got kind of quiet. I could tell from the start of the conversation that she was feeling on the edge emotionally. After a pause, she blurted out, "Ryan, babe, I'm stopping my treatments..."

Neither of us spoke for almost a full minute.

Then she added, "I'm so tired. I have no quality of life, and I just can't do it anymore."

It was like having the judge's gavel come crashing down on the table. The final sentence had been determined, and it was irrevocable. I knew that without palliative care, the days she had left would be few.

She told me not to worry. *Sure*, I thought. We cried together for a few minutes before we finally said goodbye and hung up.

I sat there in disbelief. Part of me was a little bit relieved to know she had taken the decision into her own hands, but mostly I just let the waves of devastation flow over me. She was at peace with her choice, but it was not so easy for me. I wanted her to hang on for as long as possible.

Now I knew for certain that I would lose my mom in a very short period of time, and that information was so hard to process. She was ready to go, but I wasn't ready to release her. Still, I had to live with her choice. If she was ready to go and be with the Lord, then it wasn't my place to get in the way of that grand reunion.

Through the whole final process my dad was in almost complete denial. He was still hoping for the best. He'd whisper to me, "I think she's gonna be okay; she's gonna get better." But I knew better. My medical training prepared me for what the final decline would be like. I'd seen dozens of cancer patients in their last days and knew what to expect, but Dad refused to accept the inevitable. I guess that was the only way he could deal with the impending future.

Less than two months after ending the treatments, Mom's condition came to a head. The cancer spread from her bones to her organs. Her liver and kidneys started to fail. Her belly became so swollen with fluid that she appeared to be nine months pregnant. The weight and pressure of that fluid caused excruciating pain, and she had to go to the hospital regularly to have it drained. But that was only a temporary solution. In a matter of days, the fluid would build back up again.

One morning Dad woke to find Mom semi-incoherent and hallucinating. She seemed unaware of her surroundings and was seeing what she called "chocolate balls" swarming in the air around her and dancing on the ceiling above. Dad got on the phone and called me. I told him he needed to take her to the hospital, but he stubbornly declined, saying that she probably just needed more rest and would likely be better by the afternoon.

I couldn't settle any longer for his overly optimistic reports and his unrealistic analysis of Mom's condition. I needed to see her for myself, so I got in my car and drove the seven hours to Bonanza. When I arrived, Dad had left to run an errand, and I found Mom sleeping in her bedroom. She woke up when I entered the room, so I went over to the bed. And that's when I saw it.

She had "the look." I had seen it many times in my work as a paramedic. It was the look of death. There is something indescribable in someone's eyes during their last moments on earth. Mom's eyes were sunken, dark, and lifeless.

All my emotions came surging to the surface as I knelt at her bedside. I put my head on her chest and wept, sobbing uncontrollably. I couldn't speak. I could barely breathe. Then, from somewhere deep inside Mom, cutting through all the fog and confusion, came her motherly response. She lifted her arms, placed them around me, and started gently rubbing the top of my head and the back of my neck. She whispered in my ear, "It's okay, babe. It's okay. I know. It's gonna be okay." And then she said, "You don't need to try and be strong. It's okay to fall apart."

It was already too late. I was falling apart, and my sick and dying mother was trying to console me.

Time itself seemed to stop moving, and we remained as we were, tangled together in a hug that I never wanted to end. Nothing else in the world mattered. There was only this moment between Mom and me.

While I was with my mom, my best friend, Richard, dropped by. He quickly sized up the situation. I got to my feet and staggered into his arms, weeping on his shoulder as he enveloped me in a hug. He patted me on the back and knew he didn't need to say anything. There were no words that could help.

Then, from the bed, Mom asked if I would get out my guitar and sing to her. She wanted to hear some of the songs I had written. So I got the guitar from my car and sat by the bed. I tried my best to play for her, but my tears fell on the body of the guitar, and my voice cracked with intense emotion. It wasn't much of a performance, but I think I saw her smile through her pain.

I stayed the night. The following morning Mom was disoriented again and even less responsive, so I loaded her into the car and drove her to the ER. Dad had already left for work, but he met us there. They drained her stomach and did some blood tests, which revealed a dangerously low level of sodium in her system. They administered two large sodium pills, and within 20 minutes she had perked back up. Her response was like someone switching on the lights in a darkened room.

I excused myself to go talk to the doctor. I needed the straight scoop, and he gave it to me.

"Ryan, your mom is dying. She is going to die any day. You need to get her into hospice."

I told my dad with firmness what we needed to do, and surprisingly, he was agreeable. Even he now had to admit that Mom's death was at hand.

By this point I had exhausted most of my sick and vacation time on visits with Mom, so I had to return to work in Boise. That morning before I left, I got up early and went into her room. I knelt by her bed and, with tears flowing again, told her how much I loved her. Even through her normal early morning disorientation she responded in a whisper, "I love you too, babe."

As I got off my knees I knew in my heart that this would be the last time I would see her alive.

I found Dad in the kitchen, staring into a cup of hot coffee as he stood by the sink. He set the mug on the counter, and we embraced each other. Maybe for the first time ever I saw his vulnerability and sensitivity, which were usually so well hidden, as we wept onto each other's shoulders. We didn't speak the words aloud, but we both knew that the next time I returned to Bonanza, it would be for Mom's funeral.

The call came as quickly as expected. My phone rang at 4:00 a.m., and my sister, Janay, was on the other end. She told me that Dad had called her in a mild panic to let her know that Mom was acting "strange." Janay had driven the few blocks to check on them and arrived to find Dad a little freaked out. Apparently he'd been sleeping in the bed next to her hospice bed when she had startled him awake with the question, "James, are you in here?" Her voice had sounded more normal than it had in weeks.

"Yes, Phyllis," he'd responded, "I'm here." He looked over and saw that she was not only awake, but her eyes were wide open.

Mom whispered, "Jesus is here." Then she closed her eyes and took her last breath.

Janay called me from their house to tell me this story. When morning came, Kim and I got up early and drove back to Bonanza. It was silent in the car for most of the trip. I just couldn't find any way of expressing my thoughts, and Kim respected my need for solitude. It was all I could do to fight a mostly losing battle against the onslaught of tears.

When we finally arrived at my parents' home, that walk to the front door made me feel like a prisoner on death row on the way to my execution. The house felt empty somehow without my mom, and the grief overwhelmed me. I knew that in a very real way my life was changed forever. It wouldn't be the same world without Mom in it.

The hardest thing for me in the days that followed, even as we picked out a casket and made plans for the funeral, was watching my dad barely hold it together. I couldn't face going to the viewing of Mom's body that he had arranged, and neither could Janay. We knew that this devastated corpse no longer contained the essential *her*.

We had a small graveside service with a few family and friends. It was what Mom would have wanted—a simple send-off for her departure to be with Jesus. Still, watching her shiny-new pink coffin being lowered into the ground left me with the saddest, emptiest feeling I have ever experienced. I was happy, though, that about 200 people came to pay their respects at the celebration service that followed, held at the church our family had attended for so long. It was a reminder of just how very much Mom was loved by everyone who knew her.

My mother left this earth too soon. She was only 57 years old when she died. Up to the very end she remained the person she had always been: strong, committed to family and friends, kind to strangers, her heart overflowing with love. Mom had been my spiritual rock through the years, an example of what a life of faith really looks like. She never wavered in that faith, even though she walked a difficult path in her last years.

How did she do it? I imagine Jesus had given her a special grace to walk through it; He was with her for every mile. And on her deathbed she got a glimpse of Him. He was still right beside her.

Jesus took her hand as He welcomed her home.

CHAPTER 17

DERAILED

I've heard it said, "Be careful what you pray for." In my own life I've found that God doesn't take our requests lightly—especially our requests to be changed and healed and transformed. When I had leaned against the steering wheel and prayed for Jesus to fix me and expose the lies I was believing in my heart, I had told him, "I don't care what it looks like, and I don't care what it feels like. Jesus, do whatever You need to do to heal me."

I would soon learn that God's way of answering that prayer was not what I would have expected or mapped out as His plan for me.

The months after Mom's death were difficult ones. I struggled with a deep sense that God was somehow distant. Instead of the breakthrough I had prayed for, I stood helpless as I watched my mother slowly and painfully exit this world. I'd asked Him to heal me, but instead He had taken her. It just didn't make sense to me.

Normality. That is what I wanted in my life after Mom died. I went home, continued working my shifts on the ambulance, and kept playing music. But I was so emotionally drained that I stumbled through my days in a fog of grief, confusion, and exhaustion. I was showing up for my responsibilities, but internally I was mostly checked out, limping around like a dog who'd just been hit by a car and was trying to get out of the road and to a safe place.

All the insecurities and regrets that had led to my prayer came roaring back to the surface and threatened to overwhelm me. I needed an answer to my prayer now more than ever.

After a Sunday service where I had led worship, my pastor approached me with an idea. His brother, who lived in Nashville, was a publicist for various Christian musicians, and he thought I should send some of my music to him.

Why not? I thought. I attached a couple MP3 files to an email and sent it. It couldn't hurt. Maybe this guy, Brian Smith, could at least point me in the right direction or connect me with someone who could help.

Brian was from Iowa but had lived in Nashville for years. He'd gotten his start working for a record company, then had branched out on his own, doing PR for a bunch of well-known artists. I was soon to learn what a kind and selfless guy he was—someone who was the epitome of a servant.

When Brian heard some of my music and liked it, he encouraged me to come to Nashville for a visit. He knew a guy named Martin Lovelace, who was both a local radio promoter and an artist manager, and it seemed to Brian that getting a manager would be an important first step for me. I emailed Martin and he was interested in meeting, so we set a date for me to come visit.

Finding a three-day opening in my work schedule, I booked a ticket and flew out to Nashville. It was a big step for a guy who had rarely been outside Oregon or Idaho. As soon as I touched down at the airport I could sense the vibe all around me in "Music City." This was a special place, with deep roots in all kinds of music. I breathed in the atmosphere and loved it immediately.

Martin met with me at a local Starbucks, and we hit it off right away, talking for hours about music, my goals and dreams, and my vision for singing songs that would make a difference in people's lives. The two of us really clicked. At one point he set down his cup of coffee, looked at me with an intense expression, and said, "There's definitely something here. This is the kind of stuff I look for." A few weeks later he officially became my first manager.

I was content for the time being to respond to emergency calls and drive an ambulance, but it felt like something else was beginning to take shape that would eventually elevate my musical career. I just needed to be patient. I was signed to BEC Recordings and had a manager, and one my songs was getting a good amount of national airplay. I'll never forget the first time I heard my own voice come blasting over the radio. "Yesterday, Today, Forever" was getting enough attention that I had earned a little local celebrity as the paramedic who sang Christian songs on the radio.

Even as my musical career was slowly taking shape, those old voices of shame haunted me again. Maybe the voices inside were right. Maybe I was a phony, a hypocrite, and a lost cause. Maybe I didn't deserve success. Maybe I could never be healed of all the emotional baggage I dragged along with me. Maybe if God hadn't answered that prayer by now, He wasn't ever going to do so.

When I was busy saving people's lives or making music, everything seemed okay. But the minute I was alone or lying in bed in the silence, all the darkness inside me came scrambling up to the surface. My negative thoughts were out of control, and they threatened to pull me down to a place of utter hopelessness.

I started drinking more than I should, searching for something to anesthetize the pain. At a Christmas party at one of our friend's homes, I got completely hammered and made an utter fool of myself. My words and actions turned ugly, and I managed to offend the hosts of the get-together. When I showed up to lead worship at church the next morning, I was still feeling the effects of the night before. I threw up in the bathroom and then stumbled to the stage and tried to lead worship. I was mortified by my own behavior, and I barely got through the service without puking again.

I was fooling no one.

My pastor was worried about me, so he encouraged me to get some help. I signed up for a three-day intensive conference called HeartChange, which was being held in Portland, Oregon. The trained counselors there were used to interacting with people like me, and they were ready to help me deal with my recent traumas and how I had tried to cope with them.

It wasn't easy at first, but soon I was able to open up and tell the absolute truth about my past and my present state of mind. The counselors listened intently and without any judgment. They showed me love and respect and care. As I poured out my heart, it felt so healing. As I began to confess my innermost secrets and struggles to absolute strangers, a sense of freedom began to take root within me.

I dug up all the junk within me and exposed it to the light of God, and the Holy Spirit uncovered all the lies I had come to believe about who I was. I was awakened to the power of vulnerability and how it created more trust—not less. For the first time in my life I really began to understand that God was not just my Father, but my *loving Father*. The whole experience was transformative, and it marked an important step on my healing journey.

I'll never forget sitting in the hospital room with my newborn son in my arms as Kim was lightly napping. One of the nurses was fussing around checking all the equipment. The radio was playing softly in the background. Suddenly, the DJ referred to me and introduced my song. "Yesterday, Today, Forever" started playing and the nurse looked over at me, as if asking, "Is that really you?" I nodded, and she freaked out. It was a great reminder of the reach that a song can have.

We named our son Keegan and settled down to a new sort of normal. In a short period of time we had lost my mom, gone through some major struggles in our church community, and experienced the hardship of coping with my emotional issues. It wasn't easy, and my prayer was, at best, only partially fulfilled at this point. But I felt like I had made some progress.

Kim and I knew the day was approaching for making some major decisions about our lives, but we tried not to think about that too much. Eventually, though, we came to a crossroads. I was getting a lot more opportunities to tour, and I had completely exhausted all my remaining sick and vacation days. I'd been trying to keep one foot in the paramedic world and one in the music world, but it was clear that this couldn't continue. I was weary and in need of a real vacation. But I loved playing music for people. What to do?

I had to make a choice. Devotion to the medical world, or devotion to the musical world? Though I thoroughly enjoyed my paramedic work, I knew that my heart and deepest calling had always been toward music. The paramedic work was stable and paid decently. It had great benefits and an assured retirement. There was a lot of security there. Music, on the other hand, was completely risky. There were no guarantees.

But it was a risk we both felt comfortable taking.

So, in blind faith and with no great certainty about the results, Kim and I chose music. While we didn't have certainty, we did have a strange sense of peace—a sense of rightness about our decision. We held hands, held our breath, and jumped off the edge of the cliff.

Our decision made no sense to anyone else in our lives. Everyone was puzzled and worried. Why give up a good job to chase a dream? To many it seemed reckless and irresponsible, perhaps completely foolish. But we were determined to take the step...and we did.

My first single peaked at number 12 on the Billboard Christian music charts, and I continued to get more requests to play in churches and at other events. When that song finally dropped off the charts, BEC exercised their option to release another single and sent "We Got the Light" to radio stations, focusing on the "adult contemporary" stations. The song tanked. Hardly anyone played it. It didn't make a blip on the radar. Though I was holding on to some optimism, I knew that this damaged BEC's excitement about my potential. Perhaps, in their minds, I was just a one-hit wonder…

Around the time of the epic failure of my second release, Kim found out she was 12 weeks pregnant—with twins! This caught us by surprise, but we were excited to add to our little family, even if the growth was going faster than we'd planned.

Kim had an appointment with her ob-gyn, a routine checkup, so I stayed home with Keegan while she went to see her doctor. An hour later she returned, and I knew something was wrong as soon as she stepped through the door.

The doctor hadn't been able to discern a heartbeat for either of the twins, and Kim was immediately scheduled for a procedure the next morning to remove the dead twins from her womb.

This created a fresh wave of devastation that knocked me off my feet. Honestly, Kim dealt with the news better than I did. She trusted that God had the situation in His hands. Inside, I quietly questioned how well He was holding on to us. *Maybe*, I thought, *this is a punishment for my years of sin and lack of faith.* The feelings I thought I had dealt with began to creep back into my mind and heart.

But what if this was somehow a part of how my earlier prayer was being answered? Was God taking me to the brink of despair in order to get me to trust Him?

The next morning Kim went in for her D and C procedure, and I had to board a plane for Nashville to meet up with a tour in which I was participating. I felt so guilty leaving Kim to deal with this alone, but I had no real choice. I no longer had my stable salary. Now it was all about the music, or we were going to starve.

When I arrived in Nashville, I learned that my management

company was in upheaval and that Martin was leaving to pursue other directions. Some serious financial issues meant that the company was being dissolved, and I no longer had a manager. I was on my own again, and this news came at a vulnerable time in my life. The wheels seemed to be coming off, one at a time. Thankfully, though, I still had my record deal.

I traveled around the south for the tour, and when our group got to Houston, Texas, we played a show for a big youth event. I set up my gear, we did the sound check, and then I had a little time to kill. I took a short walk and found myself sitting out on a boat dock near the auditorium where we would be performing.

My phone rang. It was my record label. I picked up, thinking they probably wanted to move ahead with a third single and were ready to discuss our strategy. Instead, after a moment of hesitation, the person on the other end informed me that the label had decided not to exercise their further options and were releasing me from the contract.

In plain language, I was being dropped. I couldn't even figure out how to respond and was silent for a long time before the voice on the other end wished me luck and hung up.

If you've ever seen those old films about nuclear bomb tests, where everything is destroyed in the blink of an eye, you'll have a sense of what this two-minute phone call did to me. A massive explosion led to a mushroom cloud, followed by a shock wave that sent ripples through me, destroying everything in its path. I was completely undone. I had no team and no support to navigate the aftermath, so I just had to let the devastation take its toll. Every voice of doubt and guilt and shame gathered in my head. They could smell the blood, like a pack of wolves closing in on a fresh kill.

I had made my choice and placed all my hopes and dreams on a locomotive that had steamed out of the station in triumph. And then, just when it had rounded the bend, it hit something immovable in its path and derailed, leaving a smoking mass of twisted and bent metal in its wake. I felt buried under a pile of rubble. That train wasn't going anywhere now.

CHAPTER 18

WHISPER IN THE WIND

The phone call from the record company felt like the last straw. What else could possibly go wrong? It seemed like I had failed in every way imaginable. Time and time again, just when I had thought that things were starting to come together, I saw my dreams drift off into nothingness.

I was afraid and confused. Now what? We had placed a bet on my future in music, but now I had neither a record company nor a manager. I no longer had a real job or the benefits that went along with it. My sweet wife had just experienced a miscarriage. My mother had died after a long and painful decline, a victim of cancer. There had been some struggles in my church, which had meant a loss of friends and fellowship. And suddenly those voices inside my head were louder than ever. I was a failure, a phony, and a hypocrite whose past still haunted him. I couldn't see any way forward.

And the God who supposedly loved me? Where was He? I felt like an abandoned child. There were so many challenges to face, and I was facing them alone.

Totally alone.

Out on that little dock, with my head in my hands, I cried so hard that it made me sick to my stomach. I felt like I was going to throw up any minute, and I had a hard time breathing. I was embarrassed by my failure. I didn't want to say anything to the other guys on tour that might just make my future even bleaker. I was angry. I was filled with fear. There was no backup plan.

In less than four hours I would be taking the stage in front of a couple thousand youth group kids. I would stand behind the microphone and deliver a message about the love of Jesus and how these kids could trust Him through every circumstance of their lives. I would tell them about how good God is—a loving Father who is there for us in every storm. I would sing of hope and the joy of a life of faith.

But in that moment none of it really seemed true to me. In my mental Rolodex I flipped through every grievance I had against God and all the disappointments I had filed away. I wasn't being paid to perform on this tour. The only income I'd get would come from selling merchandise every evening—music, T-shirts, and whatnot. So far that hadn't amounted to much. The touring was all about what I was building toward, and now that was...what?

Everything that had been bottled up inside came surging to the surface as I unloaded my bitterness and anger toward God. I screamed out loud, "Where are You? What are You doing? I knew I couldn't trust You. You don't care about me. You aren't good and gracious. You've never been a Father to me. You never had a plan for my life. You've always let me down. You've never been there for me. I don't trust You."

In that moment, I believed every word I was speaking. When I finally finished yelling at God I was utterly exhausted and physically spent. Every ounce of my energy and emotion had been expended in my indictment of Him. Surely now—if not before—God would never want to have anything to do with me ever again.

Just like David in the Psalms, I had spoken my piece. I had tossed every accusation toward God. And just like with David, God was listening. He wasn't angry, and He wasn't afraid or offended when I expressed my rawest emotions of hurt and disappointment and resentment. He understood. He knew me, blemishes and all.

Following my outburst, a gentle breeze came wafting across the water and brushed against my face. It felt like a caress. Instantly, I began to get a different perspective. That whisper in the wind was a reminder that I could trust in God and keep calm, even in the middle of the bitterest storm. The moment was so insistently and supernaturally peaceful that I felt like I was being lifted off the dock and embraced in loving arms.

I perceived a still, small voice—inaudible but very real to me—speaking through the wind. "Ah, there you are, son. There you are. I'm right here. I always have been here. I've still got you."

The voice continued, "I'm so glad that we are here together in this moment—you and Me. This is a moment that has been building since I knit you together in your mama's womb. I know that right now you don't trust Me, and you don't think I am concerned about your good. That's not true. Remember the prayer you prayed. Did you mean it?"

There was more. "I know you are in a mess and you can't see a way out of it. Your eyes only see to the horizon though. You can't see what is around the bend. I'll be waiting there for you. In this uncertain world you will always face uncertainties, but I am going to walk the journey with you. It may not be clear to you right now, but I will cause all things to work together for your good. I am in the business of making beauty from ashes, of redeeming what seems hopeless and crafting you into a work of art that shows the world My mercy and goodness. I know you are hurt and angry, but don't lose hope. I am with you every step of your journey, even through the darkest valleys and in the middle of the scariest storms.

"I love you more than you can even possibly begin to understand," the voice reminded me.

I felt a sensation that was like someone pouring warm honey over the top of my head, which oozed down my neck and spread over my tired and weary body, seeping into the hard places of my soul. In that moment the fear began to release its grip on me, and I experienced a strange and unexpected moment of peace. I had an almost surreal sense of calm. I was with God and He was with me, there in the eye of the storm.

None of my outward circumstances and challenges were any different than just moments ago, but now I knew that with God by my side I could make it through.

In the darkest moment of my life I had cursed the Lord, and His response had been to remind me of how much He loved me. I was a child held in the embrace of a heavenly Father who wasn't fazed by all my outrage. He just took me into His loving arms and held me close.

I spoke some words of confession and apologized for my attitude. I told God I was sorry for ever doubting Him. I sensed His smile.

I had a napkin with me, which I had tucked into my pocket after lunch, so I pulled it out, took a pen, and wrote down the words I'd heard in my head as a reminder of this time. I knew I might need to read them again some other day when life would seem dark and difficult. I scribbled the words on the napkin as I brushed the tears out of my eyes. "Jesus, I don't want anything coming in between You and me ever again. I don't ever want to hold anything back from You."

As I stood on the stage that evening, in front of all those young people, they couldn't ever have guessed all that had transpired in my life and heart during the last several hours. But as I sang of God's love, I meant every word. I was more convinced of it than ever before. God had answered my prayer to do whatever it would take to draw me close to Him. When everything else seemed to collapse at my feet, there He was, ready to pick me up and continue with me on the path He had chosen for me.

CHAPTER 19

FOLLOW THE RED BRICK ROAD

Several days later, I was recuperating from the first part of the tour and a nasty bout of the flu. I was drained, but I had crashed at a friend's home in the Nashville area with a peaceful sense of exhaustion. I slept for almost two days straight. Sometimes nothing is so refreshing as a long sleep.

The day before I was supposed to leave for the next leg of the tour I got an alert reminding me that I had an appointment with a cowriter that day in Franklin, Tennessee. This meeting had been set up by Martin when he was still my manager. I had forgotten all about it, and the drive would be at least 20 minutes, maybe more if the traffic was bad. I decided that I would pass, so I called Martin to let him know. Martin said, "Okay," and then I hung up.

As I collapsed back onto the couch, I once again felt a nudge and that distinct inner voice telling me, "Don't cancel. You need to do this." I let out a deep sigh and called Martin back, telling him not to cancel the meeting. I would be on my way as soon as I could put on my shoes and gather up my guitar.

I didn't want to go, but I was learning not to ignore that still, small voice. I climbed into my van and headed south to Franklin. I expected nothing of the meeting. My going was a pure act of obedience in response to that whisper in the wind I had heeded on the boat dock a couple weeks before.

I must admit that I wasn't feeling much inspiration as I drove toward my appointment. Instead, I was still feeling the ongoing effects of the flu and the aftermath of my tumultuous last couple of weeks. There were no song ideas floating around in my brain. If there had been any there before, they had been flushed away by all the emotions I had been experiencing.

I hated the idea of arriving at the meeting with nothing to offer, so I racked my brain to see if I could come up with anything. I didn't want this meeting to be a complete waste of time.

Then something popped into my mind. I had been working on a song back when our church was disintegrating under the influence of gossip, innuendo, and backbiting. All the ugly drama had led me to think about the power of words, and so I'd started fashioning a song around that concept. I'd set it aside unfinished at the time, but maybe now I could resurrect it and see where it would lead.

Most of my best songs have been born out of the experiences of my life—the struggles I've gone through, the questions I've asked, and the lessons God has taught me. These are what ignite my creativity and spark ideas that eventually make their way into my music. I'm looking to reflect on what is authentic in my own life and the lives of others, not just to pen some Christian clichés and tack on a nice tune. It takes some honesty and vulnerability to give birth to a meaningful song, but when I can manage to write with a heart wide open, I'm often surprised myself by the result.

Watching some drama unfold in my church, I had seen how words could be used to damage lives. I'd experienced words used against me like weapons—like bullets fired in my direction to try to take me down. I had also seen that words could be the agent of healing amid such struggles. Words could soothe and heal and lead to forgiveness and reconciliation. I'd seen that, for good or bad, words have the power to change the very atmosphere into which they are spoken.

At the time, I also had been reading and studying the book of Proverbs, which offers so much wisdom about the amazing power of the tongue for good or evil. I had underlined these verses in my Bible: "An offended friend is harder to win back than a fortified city. Arguments separate friends like a gate locked with bars…The tongue can bring death or life; those who love to talk will reap the consequences" (Proverbs 18:19,21 NLT). Yes, exactly.

The Bible always offers the truth about life as we live it, and as I read these words the title for a song appeared in my brain, flashing insistently to get my attention, like one of those marquees in Times Square: "Speak Life." In fact, before this phrase became a song it had become my ministry slogan and a T-shirt design. Now it had an even deeper meaning.

I'd made a few notes about this idea, but the time hadn't been right for the song to be born, so it had languished on my laptop.

As I pulled up at the location for the meeting with my cowriter, I thought someone must have given me the wrong address. Before me was an old, run-down, dingy, red brick building with muscadine vines growing up the wooden beams on the porch. It was situated next to a weary-looking gas station on the corner of an alley and surrounded by a bunch of industrial buildings and a mechanic's shop.

I checked again to make sure I had the address right. Could this really be the place? If this was a music studio of some sort, it surely couldn't be a very important one in this neighborhood.

I let out a deep sigh as I got out of my van. The belief that this was going to be a monumental waste of time resurfaced, but I also knew that I was obeying the inner voice, so I thought I would just see what happened.

Once I pushed open the darkly tinted glass doors, I remembered that old saying, "Don't judge a book by its cover." While the outside of the building was nondescript, the inside was another realm entirely. The environment was pristine and professional, but also comfortable. The walls were covered with plaques signifying number-one songs, Gold and Platinum records, and various kinds of music awards. The recording studios themselves were state of the art, equipped with all the latest technology, yet cozy and filled with light—great places for sparking the creative fire.

The first person I met was my cowriter, Jamie Moore, a shy-looking dude who reached out to shake my hand and introduce himself. He'd just been talking with the publisher, and apparently I'd been the topic of their conversation just before I had walked through the door. They had decided to cancel the meeting, but when they found out I was on my way, they decided they might as well go ahead with it.

Well, that wasn't exactly the best way to get things started.

After the publisher left, Jamie and I shared an awkward couple of minutes staring at each other and making small talk until he said, "Well, come on back." He led me down the hallway to where his little studio was tucked away. I plopped down on the couch, and we made some more small talk as we tried to get comfortable with each other. For the moment, it was clear neither of us was excited to be having this meeting.

"So," Jamie asked, "what do you want to work on?"

Okay, I thought. *Here goes.*

"Well, I have this song idea I've been working on. It's not much, and I don't have a lot written, but it's just a simple song about how our words can change the atmosphere, and I am thinking of calling it 'Speak Life.' " I then gave him a brief explanation about the events that had inspired the song.

When I wrapped up the story he had a simple response: "Cool. I love it. Let's do it."

I had a basic melody, so I played it on my acoustic guitar while Jamie started programming a scratch track. Strumming away, the song just started falling together, like a gift from heaven dropped into our laps. Working together, we hammered out the chorus and a couple verses within about half an hour, and within an hour we had added a bridge and completed our first version of the song.

It amazes me how fast songs can come together when the creative juices are flowing and I'm feeling inspired. It doesn't always happen that way. Sometimes it can take weeks for a song to take shape, but when it comes together quickly it always feels special. It was like the Lord was breathing on this one.

When we were done we both leaned back in our chairs, a little bit in awe of what we had just accomplished. We laughed aloud with pleasure, both knowing that something powerful had just been brought into being. We had caught the wave of creativity and ridden its crest.

We were excited and exhausted, so Jamie suggested we go grab something to eat and then come back and work on the song some more. We had lunch at Oscar's Taco Shop, where we scarfed down some nachos and got to know each other better.

It's wild how working creatively with someone can create a deep and powerful personal connection with them. During our two-hour acquaintance, Jamie and I had brought a new song into the world, and now it felt like we had always known each other.

Once we finished lunch we got back at it, focusing on the instrumentation and polishing the production on the track. Before I knew it, it was time to head back to Spring Hill and pack for the rest of the tour.

As we were wrapping up, Jamie walked me to the door and looked me straight in the eye. "I don't know why," he said, "but I just feel like I'm supposed to help you. I don't want money. I'd just love to write and produce with you as often as you can get here. I see it. I believe in you."

His words washed over my chapped heart like a soothing balm. I didn't even know what to say. Our time together had been incredible, and it filled me with a new hope. A couple weeks earlier my career seemed like it was over, and now I had made this beautiful connection with a talented producer. I was reminded that God could help me make powerful music that mattered and would have an impact.

As I stepped out into the late afternoon, Jamie said, "Hey man, Toby has been coming in and out of here a lot lately. I've been working on a couple songs with him, but I would love to show him this one."

Seriously? Toby? TobyMac? The same TobyMac who'd inspired me all those years ago at Jesus Northwest when I was in eighth grade? Yes, the same. Turns out that Jamie was a close friend of his and they'd been working together, producing some songs for Toby's upcoming album "Eye on It."

I kind of doubted that Jamie would actually show the song to Toby, but it certainly was a nice gesture of friendship. He was a great guy.

Two weeks later I was home from the tour and wondering what to do next. Should I go back to the world of being a paramedic...or did God still have something in store for me with music after all? I decided the wise thing would be to see if I could get my old job back, but they didn't have any full-time openings. What they did have available involved working on an "as needed" basis, which I accepted. This basically meant filling in when they needed extra help or when they needed someone to step in for overtime hours.

I was out in my garage when the phone rang. It was Jamie, and he was calling to tell me that Toby had come into the studio to work on one of his songs. When they had finished up, Jamie pulled out our session for "Speak Life" so Toby could hear it.

Toby loved it. *Loved it.* I could feel my heart start to pound in my chest.

Toby started asking questions. Jamie told him I was "this dude from Idaho who came in for a co-write." That was, honestly, about as much as he knew about me.

The line went quiet for a moment, then Jamie went on to tell me, "Toby wants to cut the song."

As I tried to keep my heart from leaping right out of my chest, Jamie went on to explain how much Toby believed in the message of the song but how he wasn't necessarily stoked about the working version we had made. He had some great ideas for changes that he thought would make it stronger, so he wanted to do some rewriting with us. I later learned that Toby had always had a desire to write a song about the power of words, but he hadn't landed on anything yet. He'd been influenced by one of Brennan Manning's books to write something like this, but now our song had dropped in front of him, and he was excited about collaborating with us.

I was initially a little hesitant about letting go of the song. After all, if TobyMac thought it was that good, then maybe it was just what I needed to resurrect my failed career. But I knew I needed to swallow my pride and let it go. So I said, "Yes, of course. Let's do it!"

"Buddy," said Jamie "you're a smart man. This is going to bless you more than you can imagine." And you know what? He was right.

In the weeks that followed, Toby was back in the studio with Jamie, re-crafting the song and meshing his own lyrics with the ones we had written. Then, with that distinct voice of his, Toby recorded his vocals and worked to give the song just the right sound. When I got a copy of the new version I was blown away. It had a new sense of presence about it. It was no longer just a good-sounding demo. It was an undeniable hit song. And how cool it was to hear Toby's voice, which I knew so well, singing a message and a perspective that I'd birthed.

I quickly discovered that you can't make much of a living from part-time ambulance service, so I began to put a lot of effort into getting gigs at churches around the Pacific Northwest. I started cold-calling churches, offering to come and play for them. Thanks to my one moderately successful radio song, I was able to get some bookings, but it wasn't enough to keep me busy full time. And since I was calling with hat in hand, I was almost always playing for a "love offering," which was never a dependable source of money. There were no guarantees. It could be dispiriting at times, but I remembered my encounter that afternoon on the dock and knew I needed to trust God and let Him lead.

There was no instant success to be found. At one point I partnered with a regional promoter in Oklahoma who wanted to book some shows for me. I was desperate, so I agreed and drove my van from Boise to Tulsa to do a three-week run of shows.

It was a disaster. My first three shows were canceled because no one showed up for them. At one of these I had to go pick up a sound system with the promoter because the venue didn't have one. For the fourth show I played for a youth group—12 kids and a few leaders. At the fifth I played for an hour and received a love offering of fourteen dollars and sold seven CDs. Oh, the glamorous life of the touring musician! My sense of disillusionment reared up again and almost suffocated me.

One night, after finishing a show with a tiny audience, I wandered back to my van with the intention of calling Kim and telling her I was giving up. I was going to face reality, quit, and come home. As I sat in my van, feeling the weight of the phone and my decision, I heard that still, small voice again: "If you can't be out here and love on these people who have nothing to offer you, then you're not ready to serve. You need to trust that I am going to provide for you."

I put the phone back in my pocket and returned to the venue to hang out with the small group of stragglers who hadn't yet left that little strip mall church in Tulsa. The size of the audience and the money earned didn't get any better for the next two weeks, but my attitude improved. I slept on couch cushions on someone's living room floor, almost always waking up with kitty litter and animal hair all over me. I also managed to survive on tuna fish sandwiches every day.

It was one nice, big slice of humble pie.

And I didn't especially love the taste.

Our finances became so tight that we had to draw out money from our 401(k)s just to get by. Trying to survive on love offerings, a bit of sporadic landscape work with my father-in-law here and there, and the very rare paramedic shift, we blew through our savings in no time at all. The whole situation was embarrassing, and our outlook wasn't very promising.

But I felt in my heart that God was in this, so I didn't give up. When I could, I would travel to Nashville to work on songs with Jamie. He continued to be unfailingly encouraging. He shared my music with anyone who would listen and told me not to lose hope. We continued to be blown away by what a good team we made together.

Another of our songs, "Holding Nothing Back," got Toby's attention. "Wow," said Toby, "that sounds like a hit!"

Jamie played my stuff for Joey Elwood, who was the cofounder (with

TobyMac and Todd Collins) of Gotee Records. Joey was intrigued to hear what I had done, but since he had just signed two new bands the timing didn't seem right. Jamie kept knocking on other doors, trying to get people to listen and telling them my story. Even though the guys from the record labels generally really liked the songs, none of them bit. They said it was great music, and then they passed.

At one point someone who worked in the radio industry spoke the unguarded truth. "Ryan, you've already been on another label, and you were dropped. You are going to be viewed as damaged goods. Since someone already tried to get things going for you and failed, no one is going to want to take the risk. You've got an uphill battle."

This was very discouraging, but Jamie and I believed we were making good music, so we kept writing songs and producing them.

My dream was still to someday be an artist on Gotee Records. I had grown up listening to bands on that label like Grits, Sonicflood, Out of Eden, Jennifer Knapp, and Relient K. But they weren't in the market for another artist—so no luck there.

One week while I was in Nashville, I met with a rep from a big label. Since the word was getting out that I had cowritten "Speak Life" with TobyMac, people were more interested in meeting with me. But their interest was in me as a songwriter, not a recording artist. Meeting after meeting went in that direction. Finally, someone had the courage to tell me what others were afraid to say.

"Ryan, I'm gonna shoot straight with you. It's not your songs. It's you. It's your voice, your look, your age. You are not going to stand out among the other male solo artists in this industry."

Ouch. I didn't know how to respond, so I just stood up, thanked him for his time, and went out to my car. I sat there in the label parking lot, alone and feeling sick to my stomach as I struggled to keep it together. If that wasn't the ultimate rejection, I didn't know what would be.

Back in Idaho, it started to look like I could get my old job back full time, but I would be losing all my seniority and, in essence, starting over from scratch. Some of the guys I had worked with were puzzled to see me again, thinking I had gotten a record deal and become a successful musician. It was humiliating to admit I had been dropped and lost everything.

One day I was out mowing my yard, listening to music on my headphones, when I realized my phone was ringing. It was the president of a small independent music company, offering me a full record deal. Of course I was excited at first, but then the doubts started to form, and I felt a nudge that this wasn't the direction I should go.

Frankly, I was getting tired of these nudges and didn't want to listen. After all, though it wasn't my dream scenario, at least I could make records. Here was a second chance. I didn't want to blow it. But I asked for a couple days to think it through and promised to get back to him.

"Sure," he said, "we love you here. We're big fans. Take as much time as you need."

Standing out there in my backyard, I felt uneasy. This was a good opportunity, but it didn't seem like the right opportunity. There was still Gotee, and I hadn't actually received an unequivocal "no" from them. It was more like, "Let's wait and see." But now I thought maybe I couldn't wait any longer.

Before I could talk myself out of it, I dialed Joey Elwood at Gotee. I was nervous, but after a few minutes of small talk I told him about the situation. I had been offered a full record deal, but in my heart, I had always wanted to be an artist on Gotee. So I wanted to double-check with him before I made the decision to go in another direction.

After hearing me out, Joey told me, "Well, bud, I was actually going to call you today, and I was dreading it because I thought we'd have a much different conversation—one that I wasn't wanting to have. I thought I'd have to tell you that Gotee wouldn't be able to get involved. That made me sad, so I was delaying the call. However, a couple hours ago, Toby called me from his car. He had been thinking about you. He said, 'If we don't sign Ryan Stevenson, we are going to miss out on something special. He is a songwriter and will always write songs. I believe in him, so do whatever you need to do to make it happen.' "

Though Joey couldn't see it from across the country, my mouth fell open. I started weeping. This was too good to be true. Unsuccessfully trying to calm my voice, I asked Joey, "Are you serious?"

"Yeah, bud. I am," he answered.

He proceeded to tell me that in the entire 20-year history of Gotee they had never signed an artist who had previously been on another label. I would be the first. He told me that he'd get the contract ready, and I should receive it within a couple of weeks.

I walked into the house, found Kim sitting on the bed, and gave her the news. With a mix of disbelief and joy we held each other and wept.

That one phone call changed everything. We had been enduring an ongoing storm for a long time, and it had shown no signs of letting up in its ferocity. All the sadness and loss and defeats had nearly overwhelmed us. But we had kept believing and hadn't given up even when all the circumstances suggested that we should.

I thought about how obedience starts with the smallest of steps. If I had blown off that Nashville cowriting meeting with an excuse about feeling sick and had never met Jamie, what would my life look like now? The road of obedience had been a rocky one, and several times it looked like failure would have the last word, but I kept on following—even when I didn't feel like I had enough faith to keep going—and God opened a new door in my life. It was a door I had knocked on since I was a teenager.

Now it swung open and invited me in.

CHAPTER 20

FRESH START

God is the God of second chances, as well as third and fourth chances. I felt like I was being given another chance after all the disappointments I had experienced. In God's own timing I had finally been given the opportunity to do what I had wanted to do for so long—give my life to making music that would touch people and heal their hearts, while at the same time being enjoyable and entertaining.

After signing the new record deal with Gotee, I signed a management deal with First Company Management, a big-time powerhouse overseeing the careers of artists such as the Newsboys. Then I began working with a booking agency to take care of my touring schedule. With all these pieces in place I could really focus on writing songs and performing them.

The missing piece was airplay on the radio. After the modest success of my first single, it had been quite a long time since my music had been in rotation. But now that a record deal had been finalized, Gotee decided to release a four-song EP entitled "Holding Nothing Back," and the title song was released as a single. The song climbed the charts and peaked at number 20 on the Billboard Hot Christian Songs chart. I was really pleased. I'd never had a song land on the AC (adult contemporary) charts before, so this was a big win and held promise that my music could reach a large audience. However, I knew by experience that one hit song wasn't enough, so I kept working at writing and recording. I was laser focused, and I kept my foot on the gas. I was determined to make the most of this unforeseen opportunity.

At the same time, I didn't want to write "for the crowd" or take the easy path with my songs. I wanted them to really mean something. I wanted to create songs that were honest and authentic, that truly reflected who I was, what I had been through, and how God had been at work in my life—not just simple little affirmations with catchy tunes. Still, I knew I needed to make sure I reached my audience. It was the balance between knowing what they wanted and delivering the message that was real for me. Believe me, trying to find that sweet spot was a learning curve. It still is.

Since music fans are always looking for something new, I could never rely on past success. I always had to fight for their attention, and there were no guarantees. The story of contemporary Christian music is littered with one-hit wonders. I was determined that I would not be one of them and was willing to work hard to continue to deliver songs that mattered.

Of course, I was also worried about my future. I had been dropped once, and I didn't want it to happen again. At times it seemed like I was walking on eggshells, cautiously tiptoeing around the challenges and hoping to keep the record company happy with me. I couldn't afford to fail. I knew there were people in the Christian music industry who, familiar with my history, fully expected me to crash and burn, and they'd scratched their heads at Gotee's decision to take me on. Proving the skeptics wrong definitely served as a motivation!

With the first single being played extensively on radio, I needed to start touring again. But this time, because of the Gotee connection, I was the opening act for some of the biggest names around: Audio Adrenaline, Newsboys, and—of course—TobyMac. During this time I ended up sharing the stage with each of the members of DC Talk, a literal fulfillment of that old dream birthed while hearing the band perform at Jesus Northwest so long ago.

The next single Gotee released was called "The Human Side," and it included some of the most honest lyrics I have ever written. Through the song I opened up about my own struggles with anxiety and lack of self-confidence as I sang, "Woke up this morning, my stomach is already in knots...Edge of my bed, struggling to gather my thoughts...I'm feeling like I'm too far gone. The hope of healing, it's already moved on."*

The Gotee team thought this raw and self-revealing song would be a huge hit, but it tanked when we released it to Christian radio. Nobody wanted to play it. I had visions of what had happened in the past when my second song for the other label failed to get traction and I was shown the door. Thankfully, things were different with Gotee. They weren't prepared to give up on me, so they remained dedicated to my career.

I continued to write, even while touring. Even though "The Human Side" had not been a success, I was still determined to craft songs with an honest intensity. I wanted to tell the whole truth about a believer's walk with God—that it isn't all smiles and flowers and happiness, that sometimes it is about recognizing Him even in the midst of pain while journeying down the hard path.

While rolling through Texas on the way to another gig, stuffed in a dilapidated old white van with my friends from 7eventh Time Down, I had an idea for a song. It spilled out of me, and I reworked it as the miles passed by on the pavement. It was called "Not Forgotten." As soon as I finished it, I knew that it was something special.

Meanwhile, "Speak Life" had become a monster hit, though not for me—for TobyMac. It hit number one on every major Christian music chart, and it stayed in that position for several weeks. Eventually it earned a Grammy nomination in 2013 for "best contemporary

---

* "The Human Side," written by Ryan Stevenson, Toby McKehan, and Jamie Moore. © 2014 Songs of Emick/Universal Music - Brentwood Benson (ASCAP)/Achtober Songs (BMI) (Admin. at Capitol CCNG Publishing.com/BMG Gold Songs/JMZL Music/Team Destiny) (Admin. by BMG Rights Management US, LLC).

Christian music song." How surreal for this country kid from Bonanza, Oregon, to share a red-carpet walk with the likes of Taylor Swift, Paris Hilton, Rihanna, Madonna, and Metallica. The song I'd written during an appointment I had nearly canceled was being honored as one of the best of the year. I only wished Mom were still alive to share the experience with me. My dad was certainly proud though.

When "Not Forgotten" was released, I know we were all feeling a little apprehensive after the failure of my previous release. We needn't have worried. "Not Forgotten" was a success, reaching number 1 for two consecutive weeks on the Billboard top-30 chart for the CHR format (contemporary hit radio). Though a less visible chart than AC, it still felt like a big win, a gust of wind in my sails, a gift from God.

Now I was ready to undertake my first full-length album. The plan was to include ten songs, including the already successful "Not Forgotten." I had plenty of material and was ready to go.

One day I was invited to join a local producer to write some songs for a new, up-and-coming artist. Because I was so busy working on refining songs for my own album, I almost turned down the opportunity. All my head space was about making my own songs the best they could be, but after thinking it over, I decided it was still worth a shot. I doubted, though, that much would come of it.

We didn't create anything special that day, but the time was worth it because that was the day I met Bryan Fowler. I didn't know it then, but that meeting would be one of the most important crossroads in my life.

Bryan was from Richmond, Virginia, and had been in a band himself, so he understood how musicians think. He was laid back, easy going, and all smiles. His carefree and seemingly lackadaisical manner created a relaxed environment, which suited me well, since I already tended to drive myself too hard. Out of this environment real creativity could flow easily. And it did.

Sometimes you don't realize you need something until you actually get it. It was that way with Bryan. Once I started working with him I couldn't imagine how I had worked without him. We were a perfect fit. The only thing Bryan lacked was some of the technical expertise in working with the engineering software, so that was all a learning curve. I remember sitting there for hours while Bryan watched instructional tutorials on YouTube to figure out how to perform a certain command we needed with the software…

It was on-the-job training for both of us, but we made a great team. Because we were all each other had, we really bonded in a special way. We were like brothers, but since we were both creative and emotional, sometimes we also fought like brothers. Creative differences could often get a little tense. But no matter how annoyed we got with each other during those long days in the studio, we would always come back together and find fresh perspectives. It was truly a case of "iron sharpens iron" (Proverbs 27:17).

With Bryan at the helm of my first full-length album, we produced a song called "Fresh Start." I didn't know it at the time, but this would prove to be an important song for me.

One morning Bryan showed up at the studio with a rather forlorn look on his face. Since he was almost always in a good mood, I knew something was wrong. When I asked, he clearly didn't want to tell me what was bugging him. I persisted, and he finally broke down and gave me the story.

He had just come from a breakfast meeting with a publisher from a local label. When asked what he was working on, Bryan told him about the album we were working on together. The publisher got a dismissive look on his face and said, "Man, I wouldn't spend a lot of time or put much effort into that project. The jury is out on whether Ryan is even an artist."

This, of course, wasn't what Bryan wanted to hear in the face of all our efforts so far. I think we were both hurt and angered by this evaluation, but we ultimately chose to brush it off and double down on proving the haters wrong.

After six weeks in the studio we were almost finished with eight more songs, and the consensus with the record company is that we'd call the record "Fresh Start." Everybody felt that it was the perfect name for an album by a guy who had made the tough climb to achieving another chance at musical success. All we needed was one more song to fill out the record.

Brad, my rep from Gotee, told me I had the freedom to write whatever I wanted. We had several potential singles already done and ready for release, so he said, "Don't write this one for radio. Write this for you." I understood that to mean that whatever this final song might be, it wouldn't ever be serviced to Christian radio. With that kind of freedom, it was easy to write from a deep place in my heart.

My thoughts went immediately to a song Bryan had shown me months earlier. While I had been out on tour with TobyMac, Bryan called me one day, excited about something he had come up with. He grabbed a guitar and played the chorus over the phone, which was all he had at that point. "Check this out," he said and then sang these words: "In the eye of the storm, You are still in control."

I loved it. We talked about finishing the song someday but put it aside for the time being.

Every time I thought about that song, though, I found myself incredibly moved. It was filled with truth that I had lived out in my life. I had found God always there with me in the darkest times. When it seemed like there was no hope, I would be reminded that He was my only hope. The song completely resonated with my own personal experience. Would it be a hit? No, I didn't think so, and clearly that wasn't the plan.

When Bryan and I finally sat down to finish the song, without the pressure of trying to create a radio hit, we decided we could just throw caution to the wind and risk doing something unique. What we created was a rugged, stomp-clap, piano-driven hymn, which talked openly about death, addiction, and financial struggles. And it was all in the context of a hope-filled, overwhelmingly positive message about trust in the only real hope giver, Jesus. It was a confession of faith in the promise that Jesus would always be there with us, creating calm in the eye of the storm while all the tempests rage around us. Our initial version of "Eye of the Storm" took shape in about 30 minutes. When we finished it, I emailed the MP3 to Toby.

Toby was on vacation, so I figured we wouldn't hear from him right away. Even when he was not on vacation he was often so busy that responding to emails wasn't always the highest priority, so we thought it would take a while to get a reply. Instead, we got a response within ten minutes.

Toby was over the moon. "Dude," he wrote, "where did this come from? This is a single!" And if anyone knew what made a great single, it was Toby. He had an unfailing ear for a hit song. I was so glad he liked it, but I knew that it was not in the plans for this song to be a single release. It would be a strong album track, but that was all.

Bryan and I kept working on the song, fine-tuning it over the next couple of days. I asked my friend Gabe Patillo if he'd be willing to come into the studio and record some background vocals. I thought that his super-deep, husky, grumbly, soulful voice was just what we needed to give the song a gospel choir vibe at the end.

Gabe stopped by the studio for what I thought would be a quick contribution of backup vocals and ad-libs. But the minute I heard him sing I knew we needed more from him than just background vocals. There was something about the way his voice worked with the song that just clicked, so I ended up asking him back later to sing the entire second verse and to be a featured guest.

Kim and I were driving somewhere when Bryan sent over the finished MP3. He had integrated Gabe's vocals into the mix and polished up the piece. As soon as the song arrived through email, I played it aloud for Kim to hear. We were both deeply moved, and a stream of tears came from Kim's eyes. As she wiped them away, she said, "This is your song. No doubt, *this is it*."

This powerful song, which seemed like a gift from God, so summed up our lives up to that point. Through all our storms and trials, He had been with us. That didn't mean that our trials went away, but experiencing His presence in the midst of them made all the difference time and time again. In so many ways, this song was our story. But as we were to find out, it was other people's story too.

As the record was pressed and released, the time came to release another single to follow up "Not Forgotten." The team made a collective decision to feature "All Yours" as the next single for both CHR and AC radio formats. It rose to number 4 on the CHR chart, but it barely made a dent in the all-important AC charts. We all scratched our collective heads. It felt like another devastating blow, and once again I felt some fear and panic rise.

I was asked to open for the Newsboys on their tour and provide a 15-minute set, which gave me time to play three or four songs, primarily those we were offering to radio as singles. I thought it through carefully and settled on a plan. However, on the very first night of the tour, I felt that nudge again—this time to make a small change in my set. Even though "Eye of the Storm" wasn't a radio single and was never meant to be one, it just felt like I was supposed to end my set with it. Since I had no backing tracks for it, unlike the previously planned closer, I just picked up my guitar and played it solo out there on the stage—just the simplicity of my guitar and voice.

Something happened in the room that first night of the tour. The audience was attentive and appreciative as I sang my singles, but when they heard "Eye of the Storm" they screamed and cheered in a way I had never experienced on stage. It was like I was singing *their* song and telling *their* stories, and everyone could relate to the promise and hope that the song offered. After the show people streamed to my merch table to ask the name of my final song—"that storm song," they called it—and to purchase the CD that included it.

Night after night as I shared that song, I sold out of all the CDs I had brought along. Everyone seemed to want "that storm song." And if they hadn't the time or money right then and there, they went to iTunes or other digital outlets to purchase it.

A couple weeks into the tour, Brad from Gotee called me and said there had been a huge spike in digital sales for "Eye of the Storm." Did I know what was going on? How could this be, since it wasn't out for radio? It was, in fact, the very last track on the record, buried at the tail end, but it was getting a lot of attention. I told him I was playing it as my closer every night.

Without a single bit of airplay "Eye of the Storm" had become the number-one song being downloaded in my entire catalog. Evidently the excitement it was creating in concert was making its mark.

CHAPTER 21

YOU REMAIN IN CONTROL

The music business is a strange business. We'd sent out "All Yours," and it had failed to make much of a splash. I couldn't figure out why I wasn't able to break through the barrier to real success. Increasingly, I felt like I was that old dog who kept barking at the gate but whom nobody wanted to let inside.

The record company was as puzzled as me. But in the music world, there are no surefire guarantees or formulas. If there were, everybody would be making hit records.

Thankfully, Gotee stuck by me, and they were willing to release yet another single. Even if nobody said so, this would likely be my last chance to get any significant promo on my records. We'd already lined up some candidates for the next single, but the surprising online success of "Eye of the Storm" suggested that maybe this song was worth a shot. But there was a problem.

Knowing how sensitive the Christian radio audience can be, everyone was concerned about whether the stations would play a song with such a rough and rugged sound and lyrics that talked realistically about the struggles of life, including addictions. Might the edginess get us in trouble and keep the song from getting played?

We made a hard decision. We would go back into the studio and soften it up a bit, rewriting some of the lyrics and changing the tempo. Therefore, the phrase "sold out by my friends" became "let down" and the reference to "addiction" became "sickness." Honestly, I was kind of angry about changing the words. The original lyrics told my own story better, speaking frankly of situations that Kim and I had been through. I'd earned the right to be totally authentic, right?

I groaned about it for a few days, then decided I had to let it go. I finally felt a sense of peace about the changes and hoped they would still communicate what I felt so deeply inside. I wanted as many people as possible to hear this message.

"Eye of the Storm" was released to radio in January 2016. At first, hardly anyone played it. Since it was unlike most of what they were playing, some stations didn't pay much attention to it. Some actively disliked it. One programmer even complained about it being "theologically incorrect," though he didn't elaborate how. Another said he didn't like my voice and found it annoying. But others really connected with it and gave it a lot of airplay. There seemed to be no middle ground.

Despite the hesitations here and there, the song started to get added to playlists all over the country, and the momentum built. The online sales of the single were doing fabulous. It was a song people wanted to own and play—over and over.

Three weeks from release, the song started to climb the charts. It was like a breaker had been pulled, and now the single had all the energy one could hope for. The lights were coming on.

In another four weeks came the wave—more like a tsunami. It became the number 1 song on the Billboard AC chart. Ultimately, every single Christian radio station in America was playing the song, including those who had initially criticized it. As so rarely happens in the music business, the song had taken on a life of its own.

I remember the day it hit number 1, TobyMac was the first person to congratulate me over FaceTime. It meant everything to me that my musical hero was rejoicing with me over my success. As he spoke words of affirmation and praise, I just fell apart. It had been such a long journey to get here.

Within the next few weeks "Eye of the Storm" was number one on every other remaining format—the number-one Christian song in America. There I was at the top of every list: "Eye of the Storm"—Ryan Stevenson—Gotee Records.

I felt like Tim Robbins' character in *The Shawshank Redemption*, after he crawled through the sewer, escaped his captivity, and stood with hands in the air, laughing with joy.

I felt like I could breathe again, even if for a moment. Or maybe it was that, for the first time in my music career, the future looked bright. A weight was lifted from my shoulders, and I experienced a new level of peace. I was so grateful for what the song had done for my life and how it had given me an opportunity to rest and reflect and quit striving.

"Eye of the Storm" remained at number 1 for 16 consecutive weeks, making it the biggest song of the year in Christian music. It was nominated for a Billboard Music Award and won a Dove Award for "Pop/Contemporary Recorded Song of the Year." It attained Gold status (more than 500,000 copies sold) and has been streamed more than 60,000,000 times. It continues to be in rotation at radio stations even to this day.

But none of these was the greatest measure of success.

What moved me even more were the emails and letters that started pouring in. People wrote to me about how much the song meant to them, how it had met them in the middle of their own storms, and how—for some of them—these words of hope had literally saved their lives, pulling them back from the brink of suicide. They all wanted me to know how important the song was to them, how it gave them a profound sense of hope that they could face whatever came their way. It obviously struck a chord for countless people, and its message reverberated in the deepest part of their souls.

So far I haven't had another song that has made such a splash, but I've been grateful for the number of other songs that have found a place on the radio charts and in people's hearts. To work as a Christian musician is a different kind of job—at times exhausting, and at times exhilarating; at times almost dangerously affirming, and at times filled with doubts and lack of self-confidence; at times rewarding, and at times a real sacrifice, especially for one's family. But I love it, and I can't imagine doing anything else.

There is no feeling on earth like taking the stage in front of a crowd and sharing the gifts God has given me in the most honest way I can. The roar of applause is wonderful, and when a whole room full of people join in singing along—knowing every word to the song—well, there isn't anything like that. Even better, though, are the one-on-one conversations with people whose lives have been impacted by my music, who have found a relationship with God, or inner healing, or a fresh burst of hope because of the words I sing.

What continues to keep me going is God's grace and protection. When I look back over every struggle, heartache, disappointment, failure, and moment of fear, I recognize that God has been with me through it all. And I know that He will continue to be with me. There is no promise in Scripture that our lives will be free from pain or that everything will always go smoothly. But there is the promise that He is always with us, even in the darkest storms of our lives. We can find some peace in the middle of the hardest experiences because He is there in the middle of the storm. I can't imagine living my life without the truth of that promise.

Sometimes I must remind myself that God is in control. He's brought the right people into my life at the right moments. He's led me to the right places. He's orchestrated my circumstances. With God, nothing is wasted when it comes to shaping our lives into the person He calls us to be. So many times I could have given up when life turned bleak. I credit Him with giving me the strength to keep going.

I know there will certainly be more struggles, more disappointments, more times of confusion in my life. But my own song will always be a reminder to me that I am not walking this journey alone.

Perhaps the most important truth I have learned is that God can be trusted—because He is good. And the way I know His goodness is through knowing His love. For too many years I thought God was kind of temperamental and looking for an excuse to be angry and disappointed with me. I believed that I had to earn His love through my actions and attitudes.

Problem was, I could never begin to live up to being the kind of perfect person I thought He expected me to be. If His love and blessing were dependent upon me—well, then I was in big trouble. All my years on the performance treadmill kept me sweating and striving but getting nowhere. Instead of accepting His love, I became bitter and depressed. The idea that God loved me no matter what and that I was actually "free in Christ" seemed too good to be true.

But it is true.

I have found so much freedom in living a life of simple trust in Jesus and letting go of all my efforts to be the "ideal Christian." When I finally got to the end of myself, it was there that I discovered for the first time how much my heavenly Father really cared for me. I saw that all the accomplishments I'd made on my own journey were not because of my hard work, but because of God's grace.

Sometimes all I've needed to do was show up, trust as best as I could, and keep an ear tuned to that still, small voice inside me—a voice that speaks loud and clear even as it speaks without words. I've learned to pay attention to the nudges of the Spirit that can help keep me on track. When I mess up, which happens a lot, I know God loves me. I embrace that forgiveness and keep going. With Him life is an adventure, and what He continues to do in me is a miracle still unfolding every day.

I'm grateful for my faithful companions on this journey, who all know me so well and love me anyway—including Toby. The redeeming nature of my connection with him has been intricately woven into my journey with meticulous oversight from the Lord. To see how the Lord used Toby and his music with DC Talk to inspire my heart all the way back in the eighth grade, then divinely put us together 20 years later, is nothing short of supernatural. Toby's encouragement, belief in me, and support along the way have truly honored me beyond words.

He handed me the keys to a new door and trusted me with his platform. Not only has he been a hero, but he has become one of my best friends.

My most crucial companion has been my wife. Kim married a low-class country boy with extra-large dreams, and she believed in them… and in me. Through heartaches and trials and gut-wrenching seasons, through days when the future looked uncertain and my own attitude wasn't making it any better, she stood by me. We've believed in God together, and we've believed in each other. She is my best friend and the one who rescues me from myself. Every day she is my best human model for the love of Christ.

Most of all, I believe in the One who is there with each of us in every storm we go through, who loves us unconditionally and unwaveringly. He walks with us through the dark times and dances with us to celebrate the best moments. He is what every father is meant to be, the very model of fatherhood: tender, gracious, compassionate, slow to anger, abounding in love. Whenever He needs to be a little tough on us, it is always for our best. He is not just our heavenly Father—He is Abba, our Daddy.

When circumstances are at their worst, He does not leave us to face them alone. He rolls up His sleeves and, without hesitation, dives into the middle of every mess in which we find ourselves. He is there with us in the middle of every one of our storms.

He *is* the Eye of the Storm.

EYE OF THE STORM

When the solid ground is falling out from underneath my feet
Between the black skies and my red eyes, I can barely see
And when I'm feeling like I've been let down by my friends and my family
I can hear the rain reminding me

In the eye of the storm, You remain in control
In the middle of the war, You guard my soul
You alone are the anchor when my sails are torn
Your love surrounds me in the eye of the storm

When my hopes and dreams are far from me, and I'm running out of faith
I see the future I pictured slowly fade away
And when the tears of pain and heartache are pouring down my face
I find my peace in Jesus' name

In the eye of the storm, You remain in control
In the middle of the war, You guard my soul
You alone are the anchor when my sails are torn
Your love surrounds me in the eye of the storm

When they let me go and I just don't know how I'm gonna make ends meet
I did my best, now I'm scared to death that we might lose everything
And when a sickness takes my child away, and there's nothing I can do
My only hope is to trust You
I trust You, Lord

In the eye of the storm, You remain in control
In the middle of the war, You guard my soul
You alone are the anchor when my sails are torn
Your love surrounds me in the eye of the storm

You remain in control
In the middle of the war, You guard my soul
You alone are the anchor when my sails are torn
Your love surrounds me in the eye of the storm*

PHOTO ALBUM

My mom and her adoptive parents, Dale and Lilian

My dad, James, and family when they first moved to the Oregon coast

My dad, James, Vietnam War, 1967

My mom , 1971

My mom and dad when they first started dating

Me in the milking parlor at the dairy

My sister, Janay, and me

Shooting rodents, learning to drive in the '69 GMC pickup, 11 years old

Family trip with the DeJongs at Crater Lake

U-12 state soccer team winning third place in the state of Oregon

Fishing with Mom during the years when we were alone at home

Junior year in high school. 17 years old, JV football team

Junior year
high school, 1996

Kim and me when we first met

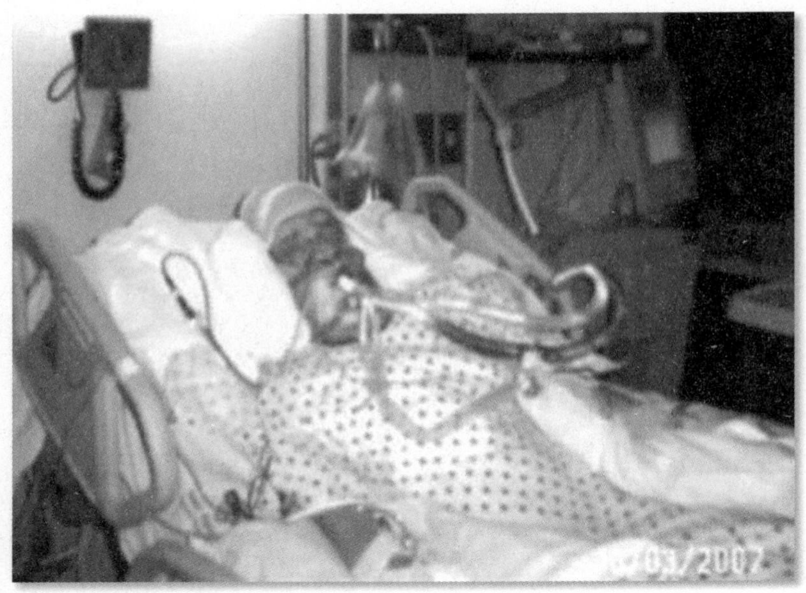

Lara in the hospital on the ventilator after the lighting strike

Lara and me at her home in Boise, post recovery

My first show with Paul at Cafe Paradiso, Eugene, Oregon (open mic night)

The day I met Toby for the first time listening to “Speak Life” in the old red brick building, 300 Franklin Road

My first tour opening for Toby!

Bryan Fowler, cowriter of "Eye of the Storm," and me

#1 award presentation for the success of "Eye of the Storm" with my label and radio team.

When I got my first Dove award for "Eye of the Storm"

Back in the ambulance bay, years after I'd left the job. Several years after signing with Gotee records

Family pic: Ryan, Kim, Joey, and Keegan

NOTES

1. William Paul Young, interview by Ian Morgan Cron, *Typology*, podcast audio, March 22, 2018, http://www.typologypodcast.com/podcast/2018/03/episode36/paulyoung.

ACKNOWLEDGMENTS

There are so many people whom I need to thank—wonderful people who have been with me in different seasons of my journey. There are too many to count, and I know I'm going to forget some of you—and for that I'm sorry. Looking back at how I've been helped, I'm so honored and reminded of how God has woven our stories together. The fact that we get to share seasons of life and memories is priceless. I'm also reminded that God does whatever He wants and uses whomever He wants. He's a master of surprise and loves to blow our minds.

To my wife, Kimberly: You are my rock, and there's simply no way I could do any of this without you. Thanks for never giving up on me—for being the best friend, wife, and momma. Love you!

To Toby McKeehan: You've been inspiring me for many years. Thank you for literally saving us and for giving me a space to grow and dream. We are forever grateful. It's been an honor to walk with you.

To Lara Eustermann; You've never owed me a thing, yet your generosity, love, and support have changed my life. I'm so happy we met that day on the side of a stormy hill. The Lord has used you in profound ways—not only to reach so many people, but to change me. Love you!

To Bryan Fowler; Thanks for bringing this song to me. It wouldn't exist without you. I'm so grateful for your friendship and how we've been able to walk together through exciting and intense seasons these last several years. We have a special bond that I cherish, and I'm forever grateful to create music with you that touches the world!

To my family (Mom and Dad—Phyllis and James—and Janay). Dad and Janay, I love you so much! Mom, I wish you were here; I hope I make you proud...

To my editor, Terry Glaspey, who shaped and smoothed my words, and to my entire Harvest House family. It's been a blast working together!

Also, special thanks to Sandy and Bill DeJong and Richard, Willem, and Susie; Greg and Evelyn Thomas; Chris and Michele Marsden; Joey Elwood; Brad Moist; Paul Wright; Paul Young; Damon Thompson; Ray Hughes; Bryan Fowler; Gabe Patillo; Chris Hauser; Matt Ingle; Chris Stevens; Brian Smith; Martin Lovelace; Dave Wagner; Derek Bruner; Wes Campbell; Mike McCloskey; Ben Courson; Lee Raner; Tyson Paoletti; Scott Huie; Ken Brown; Steve Marlow; Ada County Paramedics; Northwest Christian University; Jeremy "Jerry" Wilson; Jeff "Pru" Pruitt; Mandy "Dizzle" Barnes (yes, Mandy, I said "Barnes"); Ian Townend; Scott Pergande; and my Christian radio family all over the country.

ENGAGE WITH RYAN

www.ryanstevensonmusic.com

Twitter: @ryansmusic

Instagram: @ryansmusic